MW01710542

Making Gluten-Free Living Easy!

Cecelia's Marketplace

Kalamazoo, Michigan

www.ceceliasmarketplace.com

Gluten/Casein/Soy Free

Grocery Shopping Guide

2008 / 2009 Edition

Dr. Mara Matison
Dainis Matison

Kal-Haven Publishing

Cecelia's Marketplace

Gluten/Casein/Soy-Free Grocery Shopping Guide

by Dr. Mara Matison & Dainis Matison

khP

Kal-Haven Publishing
P.O. Box 20383
Kalamazoo, MI 49019 U.S.A.

Copyright © 2008 by Dr. Mara Matison & Dainis Matison

All rights reserved. No part of this book may be reproduced or transmitted in any form or by any means, electronic or mechanical, including photocopying, recording or by any information storage and retrieval system, without written permission from both of the authors.

ISBN 978-0-9794094-3-1

First Edition 2008 / 2009

Printed in the United States of America
Cover illustration: Lilita Austrins

CONTENTS

About the Authors

The co-author of this book, Dr. Mara Matison, received her Doctor of Dental Surgery degree from University of Detroit Mercy, and her Bachelor of Arts degree in Psychology from Villanova University. Her husband and co-author, Dainis Matison, received his Master of Science degree in Information Technology and Bachelor of Arts degree in Finance from Ball State University. They are both members of Celiac Disease Foundation, Celiac Sprue Association, Gluten Intolerance Group, and Talk About Curing Autism. These are nationwide organizations that support people with celiac disease, food intolerances, food sensitivities and autism.

Cecelia's Marketplace was established by both Mara and Dainis in 2006, soon after Mara was diagnosed with celiac disease. The couple struggled with Mara's huge lifestyle change, which included adhering to a strict gluten-free diet. Shopping trips to the grocery store were very frustrating. Spending time calling food manufacturers to find out if products were gluten-free seemed like a daily routine. They knew there had to be an easier way, so they decided to compile a gluten-free grocery shopping guide. Since then, Mara has also been diagnosed with a casein and soy intolerance, which brought about the need for the *Gluten/Casein-Free Grocery Shopping Guide* and the *Gluten/Casein/Soy-Free Grocery Shopping Guide*.

Thanks to all three of Cecelia's Marketplace Grocery Shopping Guides, grocery shopping now has become easier for not only Mara and Dainis, but also their families, friends and thousands of grocery shoppers nationwide.

Preface - Note to the Reader

Cecelia's Marketplace Gluten/Casein/Soy-Free Grocery Shopping Guide has been written to help people that are in search of gluten-free, casein-free and soy-free (GFCFSF) products. Whether you are on a GFCFSF diet, prepare GFCFSF meals for yourself or others, or just enjoy eating GFCFSF foods, this book is for you. It will help guide you to easy grocery shopping and eliminate the frustration and headaches that you've experienced trying to find GFCFSF products. This guide is also great for restaurant owners, chefs, dieticians, family members, husbands, wives, friends, and others who shop for, or prepare GFCFSF foods. For those that are not familiar with GFCFSF cooking or GFCFSF dining out, we have included three sections in the front of the book: *'What is Gluten, Casein & Soy', 'Clean Kitchen Tips', and 'Gluten/Casein/Soy-Free Dining Out'*.

We have alphabetized our *Gluten/Casein/Soy-Free Grocery Shopping Guide* to help you quickly find brand names of the GFCFSF products. The guide is easy to use: just pick a product, look it up, and you'll have GFCFSF brands at your fingertips. This book is small enough so that it can be carried with you to the grocery store when searching for products. Use it anytime, anywhere. In addition to the grocery shopping guide, there is a section in the back of the book that lists GFCFSF over the counter (OTC) medications. GFCFSF shopping has never been easier. Treasure this book and enjoy all the GFCFSF foods that are available!

Due to periodic changes in ingredients and new products, *Cecelia's Marketplace Gluten/Casein/Soy-Free Grocery Shopping Guide* will be updated annually. Look for the new edition every year.

A percentage of our proceeds are donated to nationwide nonprofit organizations that support people with celiac disease, gluten intolerance, autism, and other food sensitivities.

Dr. Mara Matison
Dainis Matison

Acknowledgments

There are many people that have contributed to the creation of this book. The support from our family and friends has made this journey more enjoyable. Lilita A. for editing, cover illustration, and all the gluten/casein/soy-free meals that kept us going; Mik for editing, critiquing and successful business strategies; Ray for editing, all the reference materials and guidance to becoming successful entrepreneurs; Ligita for editing, supporting us and all the delicious gluten/casein/soy-free recipes along the way; Lija for online advertising, data collection, editing, packaging, and shipping; Lilita M. for showing us 'The Secret'; Liana for the data collection and gluten/casein/soy-free goodies; Lauma for material support; Velta and Ilga for believing in us; Annette & Jessica Hensley, Michelle & Gloria Rutan, Ksenija Broks, Leah Gorske, and Dyani Barber for data collection; Jonnie Bryant for all the publishing advice and knowledge; Dr. Heidi Gjersoe for all the recommendations, diagnosis, and support; Larisa Kins for book page layout & cover design; Jeff Matson at Creative Group for logo design; Natural Health Center for the wonderful gluten-free book signing events; Dr. Arnis Pone, Dr. Jason Ham, Kal-Haven Publishing, McNaughton & Gunn, and all our fellow "celiacs" for all the support.

Warning - Disclaimer

This book has been prepared for the gluten-free, casein-free and soy-free (GFCFSF) consumer in order to make GFCFSF grocery shopping easier.

This book should be used as an aide to guide the GFCFSF consumer in the right direction. The content of this book is not medical advice nor is it the advice of medical professionals. The authors, Cecelia's Marketplace, and Kal-Haven Publishing shall have neither liability, nor responsibility to any person or entity with respect to gluten, casein or soy ingestion or any health consequence.

Every effort has been made to make this gluten/casein/soy-free grocery shopping guide as complete and accurate as possible. However, there may be errors, both typographical and in content. This guide should be used only as a general guide, not as the ultimate source for GFCFSF information. Food companies and manufacturers indicate that product ingredients may change periodically; therefore, the consumer needs to always check the ingredients on the manufacturers' labels before consuming their products. For specific questions or further information on a gluten/casein/soy-free diet, please consult your physician.

If you do not wish to be bound by the above, you may return this book to the publisher within 30 days of purchase for a full refund.

What is Gluten, Casein & Soy?

Gluten is a special type of protein that is most commonly found in wheat, rye, and barley. It is comprised of two main protein groups: gliadins, and gluteins. People who have celiac disease, gluten intolerance, or gluten sensitivity may suffer from chronic digestive problems when ingesting foods that contain gluten. Gluten is found in most cereals, breads, pastas, soups, and pizza crusts. It may also be hidden in foods such as seasonings, salad dressings, sauces, additives and natural flavors.

Casein is a protein found in milk. It is a phosphoprotein, which is a collection of proteins bound to phosphoric acid. Casein is found in products containing milk, such as cheese, butter, cream, yogurt, ice cream and any other derivative of milk. Many people suffering from celiac disease, gluten/casein intolerance, and autism cannot properly digest this protein.

Soy is derived from the soybean, also called the soya bean. Common forms of soy include soy meal, soy flour, soy milk, soy sauce, tofu, textured vegetable protein, tempeh, soy lecithin and soybean oil. About 9% of children in the USA are allergic to soybean proteins[1]. Various studies show that most soy allergic individuals may safely eat products that contain soy lecithin and soybean oil, since they do not contain the soy protein. On the contrary, other studies show that any form of soy should be avoided for those individuals with either a soy intolerance or soy allergy.

1. http://en.wikipedia.org/wiki/Soybean

Clean Kitchen Tips

It is very important prior to preparing a gluten-free, casein-free, and soy-free (GFCFSF) meal, to clean the surrounding area including, pots, pans, utensils and any other items being used. Bread crumbs, flour particles or other gluten, casein or soy containing foods left in the cooking area can potentially contaminate a GFCFSF meal.

Here are some tips to help prevent gluten, casein and soy contamination:

- Use an uncontaminated sponge to wash all working surfaces with soap and water.
- Clean and inspect pots, pans, utensils, cutting boards and other kitchenware for gluten, casein or soy residue.
- Use clean kitchen hand towels.
- If grilling, place aluminum foil over the grilling area.
- Use squeeze bottle mustard, ketchup, peanut butter, jelly/jam, or other condiments to prevent cross-contamination.
- Avoid using wooden utensils. Gluten, casein and/or soy residue can stay embedded in wooden utensils and cutting boards.
- Use a separate toaster for GFCFSF bread, rice cakes, etc..
- In commercial kitchens, if using latex/rubber gloves, make sure the gloves are not coated with powder (starch).
- Do not deep fry foods in contaminated oil (i.e. from breaded chicken wings, breaded chicken tenders, mozzarella sticks).

Gluten/Casein/Soy-Free Dining Out

Nationwide restaurant chains offering *gluten-free menus:

Biaggi's Ristorante
Bonefish Grill
Bugaboo Creek Steakhouse
Carino's Italian Grill
Carraba's Italian Grill
Charlie Brown
Cheeseburger in Paradise
Claim Jumper
Fleming's Prime Steakhouse & Wine Bar
Old Spaghetti Factory
Outback Steakhouse
P.F. Chang's China Bistro
Pasta Pomadoro
Pei Wei Asian Diner
Weber Grill Restaurant
Wildfire Restaurants
Z. Tejas Southwestern Grill

*These menus are only gluten-free. Please explain to the wait staff that the meal needs to be gluten-free and also casein-free and soy-free.

Our Data Collection

The product information in this book was collected between June 2008 - August 2008. The information was received from product manufacturers and major supermarkets via internet, e-mail, phone or mail.

The Food and Drug Administration (FDA) has proposed to define the term "gluten-free" as containing less than 20 parts per million (ppm) gluten. This regulation was scheduled to be issued in 2008. Some food manufacturers have already begun testing their products for the presence of gluten. Those products that have not passed this test have been excluded from this book. Currently, not all companies test their products, therefore, we cannot guarantee that all the products listed in our book are less than 20 ppm gluten.

Casein is the protein found in milk products. Milk is one of the top eight allergens recognized by the FDA. Products containing any form of milk have been excluded from this guide. This includes casein, caseinate, lactose, or any other milk derivative.

Soy is also one of the top eight allergens recognized by the FDA. Products containing any form of soy have been omitted from this guide, including soy lecithin and soybean oil.

Those products that have been manufactured in the same facility as gluten, casein or soy, but indicate that they thoroughly wash their lines between products have been included. We have tried our best not to include products from manufacturers that do not take measures to prevent cross-contamination.

For more information on our data collection and up to date product alerts, please visit our website www.ceceliasmarketplace.com.

Other Products Available
by Cecelia's Marketplace

BOOKS:

Grocery Shopping Guides:
Gluten-Free
Gluten/Casein-Free

Safety Labels:

Gluten-Free Safety Labels

For **Product Alerts** or more information about our products please visit us online:

www.CeceliasMarketplace.com

This book is dedicated to:

All those in search of gluten/casein/soy-free products.

To help conserve our environment this book has been printed on recycled paper (30% post consumer waste).

Gluten/Casein/Soy-Free Grocery Shopping Guide (A-Z)

A

Acorn Squash... see Squash
Almonds... see Nuts
Amaranth
- **Arrowhead Mills** - Whole Grain
- **Bob's Red Mill** - Organic Flour
- **Nu-World Foods** -
  - Bread Crumbs
  - Flour
  - Pre Gel Powder
  - Puffed
  - Seed
  - Side Serve (Garlic Herb, Savory Herb, Spanish Tomato)
  - Starch
  - Toasted Bran Flour

Anchovies
- **Crown Prince** - Flat, Rolled

Angel Hair Pasta... see Pasta
Apple Butter
- **Eden** - Organic (Apple, Apple Cherry)

Apple Cider... see Cider
Apple Cider Vinegar... see Vinegar
Apples... *All **Fresh** Apples Are **Gluten/Casein/Soy-Free***
Applesauce
- **365 Organic Every Day Value** -
  - Cinnamon, Unsweetened
- **Baxters** - Bramley Apple Sauce
- **Del Monte Nature's Goodness Baby Food** -
  - Applesauce (Stage 1, Stage 2, Stage 3)
- **Eden** - Apple, Apple (Cherry, Cinnamon, Strawberry)

Great Value Brand (Wal-Mart) -
- Applesauce Glass Jar
  - Cinnamon
  - Regular
  - Unsweetened
- Applesauce Plastic Cups
  - Cinnamon
  - Natural
  - No Sugar Added
  - Regular
- Regular Canned Applesauce

Hy-Vee -
- Applesauce
- Cinnamon
- Natural (Unsweetened)

Kroger Brand - Flavored, Plain

Meijer -
- Chunky
- Cinnamon
- Mixed Berry
- Natural
- Organic
  - Cinnamon
  - Sweetened
  - Unsweetened
- Regular
- Strawberry

Mott's - All Varieties

Musselman's -
- Chunky
- Cinnamon (Lite, Regular)
- Homestyle

Unsweetened

Publix - Cinnamon, Old Fashioned, Unsweetened

Safeway Brand - Cups, Natural, Sweetened

Spartan Brand -

Cinnamon

Natural

Peach

Raspberry

Regular

Strawberry

Sunny Select - Original

Wegmans Brand -

Applesauce

Cinnamon

Mixed Berry

Peach Mango

Natural Applesauce

Chunky

Regular

Sweetened Applesauce

Chunky

MacIntosh

Regular

Whole Kids Organic -

Mixed Berry

Organic Apple

Peach

Strawberry Banana

Woodstock Farms -

Organic Applesauce

Apricot

Blueberry

Cinnamon
Mango
Regular
Apricots... **All **Fresh** Apricots Are **Gluten/Casein/Soy-Free***
Del Monte -
Canned Fruit (All Varieties)
Fruit Snack Cups (All Metal & Plastic Containers)
Hy-Vee - Unpeeled Halves (Regular)
Meijer Brand - Halves Unpeeled In Pear Juice
S&W - All Varieties
Sunny Select - Canned
Wegmans Brand - Canned Halves
Artichokes... **All **Fresh** Artichokes Are **Gluten/Casein/Soy-Free***
365 Every Day Value - Artichoke Hearts
Native Forest -
Artichoke Hearts
Marinated
Quartered
Whole
Reese -
Artichoke Heads
Extra Small
Medium
Petite
Quartered Bottoms
Small
Trader Joe's - Artichoke Hearts In Water
Wegmans Brand -
Artichoke Hearts
Halves & Quarters
In Brine

Asparagus... **All **Fresh** Asparagus Is **Gluten/Casein/Soy-Free***

Birds Eye - All Frozen Asparagus ***(Except With Sauce)***

Cascadian Farm - Organic Frozen Asparagus Cuts

Del Monte - All Varieties

Great Value Brand (Wal-Mart) -

Canned (All Green Asparagus Spears, Cuts & Tips, Extra Long)

Frozen (Whole Spear Asparagus)

Meijer Brand - Canned Cuts & Tips

Native Forest -

Green (Cuts & Tips, Spears)

White

S&W - All Varieties

Spartan Brand - Cut

Wegmans Brand - Cut Green Spears & Tips

Woodstock Farms - Organic Frozen Whole Baby Asparagus

Avocado... **All **Fresh** Avacodos Are **Gluten/Casein/Soy -Free***

Avocado Dip... see Dip

B

Baby Food

Beech-Nut -

Stage 1 Fruits

Applesauce

Chiquita Bananas

Peaches

Pears

Prunes

Stage 1 Meats

Beef & Beef Broth

Chicken & Chicken Broth
Turkey & Turkey Broth
Stage 1 Vegetables
Butternut Squash
Tender Golden Sweet Potatoes
Tender Sweet Carrots
Tender Sweet Peas
Tender Young Green Beans
Stage 2 Dinners
Apples & Chicken
Chicken & Rice
Chicken Noodle
Homestyle Chicken Soup
Macaroni & Beef w/Vegetables
Pineapple Glazed Ham
Sweet Potatoes & Chicken
Turkey & Rice
Vegetables & Beef
Vegetables & Chicken
Stage 2 Fruits
Apples & Bananas
Apples & Blueberries
Apples & Cherries
Apples & Pears
Apples w/Mango & Kiwi
Apples w/Pears & Bananas,
Applesauce
Apricots w/Pears & Apples
Chiquita Bananas
Chiquita Bananas & Strawberries
Chiquita Bananas w/Pears & Apples
DHA Plus Apple Delight

- Guava
- Mango
- Papaya
- Peaches
- Peaches & Bananas
- Pears
- Pears & Pineapples
- Pears & Raspberries
- Plums w/Apples & Pears
- Prunes w/Pears

Stage 2 Rice Cereal (Apples w/Cinnamon)

Stage 2 Vegetables

- Butternut Squash
- Carrots & Peas
- Corn & Sweet Potatoes
- Country Garden Vegetables
- DHA Plus Garden Vegetable
- DHA Plus Sweet Potatoes
- Mixed Vegetables
- Sweet Corn Casserole
- Sweet Potatoes & Apples
- Tender Golden Sweet Potatoes
- Tender
    - Sweet Carrots
    - Sweet Peas
    - Young Green Beans

Stage 3 Dinners

- Country Vegetables & Chicken

Stage 3 Fruits

- Apples & Bananas
- Chiquita Bananas
- Pears

Stage 3 Rice Cereal & Pears
Stage 3 Turkey Rice Dinner
Stage 3 Vegetables
Green Beans & Corn & Rice
Sweet Potatoes
Table Time
Apple Dices in White Grape Juice From Concentrate
Carrot Dices
Green Bean Dices

Del Monte Nature's Goodness Baby Food

Stage 1 Fruits & Vegetables
Applesauce
Bananas
Carrots
Green Beans
Peaches
Pears
Peas
Prunes
Squash
Sweet Potatoes
Stage 2 Desserts
Banana Apple
Banana Pudding
Cherry Vanilla Pudding
Dutch Apple
Fruit Dessert
Hawaiian Delight
Mango Fruit
Papaya Fruit
Peach Cobbler

- Pink Guava Fruit
- Tutti Frutti

Stage 2 Dinners
- Apples & Chicken
- Apples & Ham
- Broccoli & Chicken
- Green Beans & Turkey
- Sweet Potatoes & Turkey
- Turkey Rice Dinner
- Vegetable Dinner
  - Bacon
  - Beef
  - Chicken
  - Ham

Stage 2 Fruits & Vegetables
- Apples & Blueberries
- Apples & Cranberries
- Apples & Pears
- Apples w/Squash
- Applesauce
- Apricots w/Pears & Apples
- Bananas
- Bananas w/Pears & Apples
- Carrots
- Corn & Sweet Potatoes
- Green Beans
- Mixed Vegetables
- Peaches
- Pears
- Plums w/Apples
- Prunes w/Pears

Pumpkins w/Pears
Sweet Peas
Stage 2 Rice Cereal w/Applesauce
Stage 3 Desserts
Bananas & Strawberry w/Tapioca
Bananas w/Tapioca
Tutti Frutti
Stage 3 Dinners
Vegetable Ham
Stage 3 Fruits & Vegetables
Applesauce
Pears
Sweet Potatoes
Whole Grain Rice Cereal

Gerber Baby Food -
1st Foods Fruits & Vegetables
Applesauce
Bananas
Carrots
Green Beans
Peaches
Pears
Peas
Prunes
Squash
Sweet Potatoes
2nd Foods Desserts
Banana Apple
Dutch Apple
Fruit Medley
Guava

B

2nd Foods Dinners
- Apples & Chicken
- Beef & Beef Gravy
- Chicken & Chicken Gravy
- Chicken & Rice
- Sweet Potatoes & Turkey
- Vegetable Beef
- Vegetable Chicken

2nd Foods Fruits & Vegetables
- Apple Strawberry Banana
- Apples & Cherries
- Applesauce
- Apricots w/Mixed Fruit
- Banana Mixed Berry
- Banana Orange Medley
- Banana Plum Grape
- Banana w/Apples & Pears
- Bananas
- Carrots
- Garden Vegetable
- Green Beans
- Peaches
- Pear Pineapples
- Peas
- Squash
- Sweet Potatoes
- Sweet Potatoes & Corn

3rd Foods Desserts
- Fruit Medley Dessert

3rd Foods Dinners Vegetable
- Beef
- Chicken

Turkey
3rd Foods Fruits & Vegetables
Applesauce
Banana Strawberry
Bananas
Carrots
Green Beans w/Rice
Peaches
Pears
Squash
Sweet Potatoes
Gerber Organic Baby Food -
1st Foods
Applesauce
Bananas
Carrots
Pears
Sweet Peas
Sweet Potatoes
2nd Foods
Apple Strawberry
Applesauce
Bananas
Butternut Squash & Carrots
Chicken & Wild Rice
Corn
Green Beans
Pear & Wildberry
Squash Corn & Chicken
3rd Foods
Tender Harvest Savory Carrots Potatoes Beef

Mini Fruits
- Apple Strawberry
- Banana Mango

Meijer Brand -
- Gluco Burst (Arctic Cherry)
- Little Fruit (Apple, Strawberry/Banana)
- Little Veggies Corn

O Organics -
- Stage 1
  - Applesauce
  - Bananas
  - Carrots
  - Peas
  - Sweet Potatoes
- Stage 2
  - Apple Apricot
  - Apple Banana
  - Apple Wild Blueberry
  - Applesauce
  - Bananas
  - Carrots
  - Mixed Vegetables
  - Peach Rice Banana
  - Pear Raspberry
  - Pears
  - Peas and Brown Rice
  - Prunes
  - Squash
  - Summer Vegetables
  - Sweet Potatoes

Stage 3
Sweet Potato Chicken Dinner
Vegetable
Vegetable Beef Dinner

Bacon

Applegate Farms -
Canadian
Dry Cured
Peppered
Sunday (Organic, Regular)
Turkey (Organic, Regular)

Black Label - Original

Dietz & Watson -
Canadian Style
Premium Imported

Ejays So. Smokehouse -
Applewood Smoked
Canadian Style
Mesquite Smoked Pork Bacon
Jalapeno
Regular

Farmer John -
Premium Low Sodium
Quick Serve (Fully Cooked)

Great Value Brand (Wal-Mart) -
Hickory Smoked
Lower Sodium

Hormel -
Canadian Style
Fully Cooked

B

Jimmy Dean -
Premium Bacon
Hardwood Smoked Turkey
Lower Sodium
Original
Thick Slice
Meijer Brand -
Lower Sodium
Regular
Oscar Mayer -
America's Favorite Naturally Hardwood Smoked
Fully Cooked Ready To Serve Bacon (Hearty Thick Cut)
Publix -
Center Cut
Fully Cooked
Lower Sodium
Original
Trader Joe's - Turkey
Wellshire Farms -
Bacon
Classic Sliced Dry Rubbed
Classic Sliced Turkey
Dry Rubbed Center Cut
Range Sliced Dry Rubbed
Range Sliced Peppered
Sliced Applewood Smoked Maple
Sliced Beef
Sliced Canadian Style
Sliced Panchetta
Sliced Peppered Turkey

Bacon Bits
Hormel - Real Bacon (Bits)

B

Bagels
- **Enjoy Life** -
  - Cinnamon Raisin
  - Classic Original
- **Kinnikinnick** -
  - Tapioca Rice
    - Cinnamon Raisin
    - New York Style Plain
    - Sesame
- **Trader Joe's** - Gluten Free Bagels

Baguettes... see Bread

Baking Chips
- **Ener-G** - Chocolate Chips
- **Enjoy Life** - Semi Sweet Chocolate Chips
- **Trader Joe's** - Unsweetened Belgium Baking Chocolate

Baking Cocoa
- **Hy-Vee**
- **Kroger Brand**
- **Spartan Brand** - Cocoa Baking Chocolate

Baking Decorations & Frostings
- **Betty Crocker** -
  - All Bottle Decors
    - Nonpareils
    - Sugars
  - Almond Paste
  - Decorating Gels (All Colors)
  - Neon Decorating Gel
- **Cake Mate** - Decorating Gels (All Colors)
- **Cherrybrook Kitchen** - Gluten Free Frosting (Chocolate, Vanilla) ***(Box Must Say Gluten-Free)***

Edward's & Sons
Food-Tek Fast & Fresh - Dairy Free Chocolate Flavored Icing
Gluten-Free Essentials -
Frosting Mix
Lemon Glaze
Supreme Chocolate
Vanilla Royal
Gluten-Free Pantry - Crisp & Crumble Topping
Let's Do...Sprinkelz
Carnival
Chocolatey
Confetti
Pamela's Products -
Frosting Mix
Confetti
Dark Chocolate
Vanilla

Baking Mix... see Bread Mix

Baking Powder
Barkat
Bob's Red Mill
Clabber Girl
Cause You're Special - Double Acting
Davis
Ener-G - Double Acting, Regular
Hain Pure Foods
Hy-Vee - Double Acting
Kinnikinnick - KinnActive
Kraft - Calumet
Kroger Brand
Rumford

B

Watkins
Wegmans Brand - Double Acting
Baking Soda
Arm & Hammer
Bob's Red Mill
Ener-G -
Baking Soda
Calcium Carbonate Baking Soda Substitute
Hy-Vee
Kroger Brand
Meijer Brand
Spartan Brand
Bananas... **All **Fresh** Bananas Are **Gluten/Casein/Soy-Free***
Chiquita
Dole
Woodstock Farms - Organic Frozen Bananas
Barbeque Sauce
Bone Suckin' Sauce -
Hiccuppin' Hot
Hot
Hot Thicker Style
Original
Rib Rub
Thicker Style
Consorzio Marinades - Organic BBQ
Daddy Sam's -
Medium Ginger Jalapeno
Original Recipe
Salmon Glaze
Homestyle Meals -
Original
Smoked Chipotle

Hy-Vee -
Hickory
Honey Smoke
Original
Mr. Spice Organic - Honey BBQ
Organicville - Original
Publix -
Hickory
Honey
Original
Saz's -
Original
Sassy
Vidalia Onion
Sweet Baby Ray's -
Hickory & Brown Sugar
Honey
Honey Chipotle
Original
Sweet 'N Spicy
Sweet Vadalia Onion
Wegmans Brand - Memphis Style, Tropical
Wild Thymes - Spicy Island BBQ Sauce
Bars... (includes Breakfast, Energy, Fruit, Protein, etc.)
123 Gluten Free - Sweet Goodness Pan Bars
Aller Energy Bars -
Apple Cinnamon
Cherry Blossom
Chocolate Swirl
Wild Berry
Alpsnack -
Apricots & Cranberries

Coconut/Mango & Pineapple
Plums & Currants

Arico -
Cookie Bars
Almond Cranberry
Peanut Butter

Boomi Bar -
Almond Protein Plus
Apricot Cashew
Cashew Almond
Cranberry Apple
Fruit & Nut
Healthy Hazel
Macadamia Paradise
Maple Pecan
Perfect Pumpkin
Pineapple Ginger
Pistachio Pineapple
Walnut Date

Bora Bora -
Almond Sunflower
Cinnamon Oatmeal
Cranberry Crunch
Peanut Peanut
Sesame Raisin

Bumble Bar -
Awesome Apricot
Cherry Chocolate
Chocolate Crisp
Chunky Cherry
Original Flavor

B

Original Flavor With
Almonds
Cashews
Hazelnuts
Mixed Nuts
Tasty Tropical
Clif Nectar -
Cherry Pomegranate
Cranberry Apricot Almond
Dark Chocolate
Mocha
Raspberry
Walnut
Lemon Vanilla Cashew
Eat Natural -
100% Organix Brazils Hazelnuts and Sulatan
Brazils Sultana, Almonds and Hazelnuts
Dates, Walnuts and Pumpkin Seeds
Macadamias, Brazils and Apricots
Peanuts Almonds and Hazelnuts
Ecco Bella -
Beautiful Bones
Instant Bliss Beauty
Ener-G - Chocolate Chip Snack Bar
Enjoy Life -
Caramel Apple
Cocoa Loco
Sunbutter Crunch
Very Berry
Gopal's -
Adam & Eve
Apple Delicious

B

Ayurvedic
Carob Quinoa
Happy Herb
Pineapple Nut
Pumpkin Agave
Rawmesan
Sesame Mango
Walnut Fig

Larabar -
Apple Pie
Banana Cookie
Cashew Cookie
Cherry Pie
Chocolate
Cherry
Coconut
Coffee
Hazelnut
Mint Orange
Regular
Cinnamon Roll
Cocoa Mole
Coconut Cream Pie
Ginger Snap
Key Lime Pie
Lemon Bar
Peanut Butter Cookie
Pecan Pie
Pistachio

Mrs. May's Naturals -
Trio
Blueberry

Cranberry
Strawberry
Tropical

Nutiva Bars -
Flax & Raisin
Hempseed

Omega Smart Bars -
Banana Chocolate Chip
Pomegranate Strawberry Colada
Pumpkin Spice

Organic Food Bar -
Organic Food Bar
Active Greens
Cranberry
Omega 3 Flax
Original
Protein
Vegan
Wild Blueberry
Organic Food Bar Kids
Apple Pie
Cherry Pie
Chocolate Brownie Crunch
Raw Organic Food Bar
Cinnamon Raisin

Oskri Organics -
Coconut Bar
Almond
Cherry
Mango
Original

Pineapple
Strawberry
Date
Fig
Fruit
Honey Bar
Cashew
Desert Delight
Flaxseed
Granola
Mixed Nuts
Muesli
Turkish Delight
Jalow
Almond Cranberry
Cashew Cranberry
Pecan Raisin
Sesame Bar
Black Sesame
Date Syrup &
Black Cumin
Fennel
Regular
Molasses &
Black Cumin
Fennel
Regular
Quinoa
PURE Bar -
Organic
Apple

B

Cinnamon
Cherry Cashew
ChocChip Trailmix
Chocolate Brownie
Cranberry Orange
Wild Blueberry

Ruth's Hemp Power -
Flax Power
CranNut
Tropical
Very Berry
Maca
Ginger Almond
Lemon Hazelnut

Seitenbacher - Xtra Fiber

thinkOrganic -
Apricot Coconut
Cashew Pecan
Cherry Nut
Chocolate Coconut
Cranberry Apple
Tropical Nut

Wegmans Brand -
Fruit Flats
Cherry
Grape
Raspberry
Strawberry

Basmati Rice... see Rice

Bean Dip... see Dip

Beans... **All* ***Fresh*** *Beans Are* ***Gluten/Casein/Soy-Free (Except Soybeans)***

365 Every Day Value -
- Cannellini
- No Salt Added
  - Black
  - Cut Green
  - Garbanzo
  - Kidney
  - Pinto

365 Organic Every Day Value -
- Frozen Cut Green

Amy's -
- Refried Beans
  - Black (Light In Sodium, Regular)
  - Traditional (Light In Sodium, Regular)
  - w/Green Chiles
- Vegetarian Baked

Arrowhead Mills -
- Adzuki
- Anasazi
- Garbanzo (Chickpeas)
- Green Split Peas
- Lentils (Green, Red)
- Pinto

B&M Baked Beans -
- Baked Beans
  - BBQ Flavored
  - Bacon & Onion
  - Country Style
  - Maple Flavor
  - Original

Vegetarian
Red Kidney
Birds Eye - All Frozen Green Beans ***(Except With Sauce)***
Bush's Best -
Baked Beans
Boston Recipe
Country Style
Homestyle
Honey
Maple Cured Bacon
Onion
Original
Vegetarian
Black
Frijoles Negros Condimentados
Regular
Cannellini
Garbanzo
Great Northern
Kidney
Dark Red
Light
Microwaveable Cup Original
Pinto
Frijoles Pintos
Cascadian Farms -
Organic Frozen
Cut Green Beans
French Cut Green Beans w/Toasted Almonds
Petite Whole Green Beans
Del Monte - All Varieties ***(Except Del Monte Savory Sides Green Bean Casserole)***

Eden -
- Organic
  - Aduki
  - Baked w/Sorghum & Mustard
  - Black
  - Black Eyed Pea
  - Cannellini
  - Caribbean Black
  - Garbanzo
  - Great Northern
  - Kidney
  - Navy
  - Pinto
  - Small Red
- Refried
  - Black
  - Kidney
  - Pinto
  - Spicy Black
  - Spicy Pinto
- Rice &
  - Cajun Small Red
  - Caribbean Black
  - Garbanzo
  - Kidney
  - Lentils
  - Pinto

Fantastic World Foods -
- Hummus Original
- Instant
  - Black
  - Refried

B

Freshlike -

Frozen Plain Green Beans ***(Except Pasta Combos and Seasoned Blends)***

Great Value Brand (Wal-Mart) -

Canned Beans

Cut Green

Fat Free Refried

French Style Green

No Salt Added

Cut Green

French Style Green

Pinto

Red

Whole Green

Dried Beans

Baby Lima

Black

Garbanzo

Great Northern

Large Lima

Light Red Kidney

Navy

Pinto

Small Red

Dried Lentils

Dried Peas

Blackeye

Chick

Green Split

Frozen

Baby Lima

Cut Green
French Style Green

Green Giant -

Canned
Cut Green (50% Less Sodium, Regular)
French Style Green
Kitchen Sliced Green

Frozen
Cut Green
Select w/No Sauce Whole Green

Hy-Vee -

Baby Lima
Black (Refried, Regular)
Blue Lake
Cut Green
French Style Green
Whole Green
Cut Green
Dark Red Kidney
Fat Free Refried
Garbanzo Beans Chick Peas
Great Northern
Home Style Baked
Large Lima
Lentils
Light Red Kidney
Navy
Onion Baked
Original Baked
Pinto
Pork & Beans

Red (Kidney, Regular)
Traditional Refried

Joan of Arc -
Dark Red Kidney
Light Red Kidney

Kroger Brand - Unseasoned (Canned, Dry)

Meijer Brand -
Baked Beans - Organic
Canned Beans
Black (Organic, Regular)
Butter
Garbanzo (Organic, Regular)
Great Northern
Lima
Mexican Style
Pinto (Organic, Regular)
Red Kidney
Dark
Dark Organic
Light
Regular
Refried
Fat Free
Regular
Vegetarian
Refried Organic
Black Bean
Black Bean/Jalapeno
Roasted Chili/Lime
Traditional
Wax (Cut)

Canned Green Beans Cut
Blue Lake
French Style
Blue Lake
No Salt
Organic
Veri Green
No Salt
Organic
Veri Green
Canned Green Beans Whole
Frozen Green Beans
Cut
French Cut
Italian Cut
Frozen Lima Beans
Baby
Fordhook
Pork & Beans
Midwest Country Fare -
Cut Green
French Style
Frozen Cut
Pork & Beans
O Organics -
Canned
Black
Garbanzo
Kidney
Pinto
Pictsweet - All Plain Green Beans (Frozen)

Publix -
- Canned
  - Baked
  - Green (Veggi Green)
  - Kidney (Dark, Light)
  - Pork & Beans
- Dry
  - Baby Lima
  - Black
  - Blackeye
  - Garbanzo
  - Great Northern
  - Large Lima
  - Lentils
  - Light Red Kidney
  - Navy
  - Pinto
  - Small Red
- Frozen
  - Green (Cut, French Cut)
  - Lima (Baby, Fordhook)

Safeway Brand -
- Canned
  - Black (Eyed, Regular)
  - Chick Peas
  - Dark Kidney
  - Green
  - Light Kidney
  - Lima
  - Pinto
- Chili (Mexican Style)

- Dried
  - Baby Lima
  - Black (Eyed, Regular)
  - Great Northern
  - Green Split
  - Large Lima
  - Lentils
  - Light Red Kidney
  - Navy
  - Pink
  - Pinto
  - Small (Red, White)
- Refried Beans

Spartan Brand -

- Canned
  - Baked
    - Regular
    - w/Bacon & Maple Flavor
    - w/Onions
  - Black
  - Butter
  - Dark Red Kidney
  - Garbanzo
  - Great Northern
  - Green
    - Cut
    - French Cut French Style
  - Homestyle Baked
  - Light Red Kidney
  - Pinto

Pork & Beans
Red
Refried
Regular & Fat Free
Wax
Whole Green
Dried
Baby
Black
Black Eyed
Great Northern
Kidney
Lentil
Lima (Baby, Large)
Navy
Pinto
Frozen
Baby Lima
Cut Green
Fordhook Lima
French Cut Green
Speckled Butter
Whole Green
Refried Beans
Fat Free
Regular
Sunny Select -
Canned Black
Green Beans (Canned, Frozen)
Refried (Fat Free, Regular, Vegetarian)

Wegmans Brand -
- Baby Lima
- Baked Beans (Homestyle, Vegetarian)
- Black
- Butter
- Cannellini Beans Italian Classics
- Cut Green Beans (No Salt, Regular)
- Dark Kidney
- Dark Red Kidney No Salt Added
- Fordhook Lima
- French Style Green Beans (No Salt, Regular)
- Garbanzo Beans Italian Classics
- Great Northern
- Green
  - Cut
  - French Style
  - Italian
  - Regular
  - Whole
- Light Kidney
- Lima
- Pinto
- Pork & Beans In Tomato Sauce
- Veggi Green Cut Green
- Wax

Woodstock Farms -
- Organic Frozen
  - French Beans
  - Cut Green Beans
  - Lima

B

Beef... **All **Fresh** Meat Is **Gluten/Casein/Soy-Free** (**Non-Marinated, Unseasoned**)*

Applegate Farms -
- Deli
  - Peppered Eye Round
  - Roast Beef
- Organic Roast Beef
- Sliced Roast Beef

Dietz & Watson -
- Cooked Corned Beef (Extra Lean)
- Corned Beef Brisket
- Roast Beef
  - Angus
  - Choice
  - London Broil
  - Pepper Choice Eye Round
  - Trim & Tied

Great Value Brand (Wal-Mart) -
- Frozen (100% Pure Beef Patties)

Homestyle Farms -
- Bulk Beef BBQ Cooked
- Shredded Beef In BBQ Sauce

Hy-Vee -
- Quarter Pounders
- Thin Sliced
  - Corned Beef
  - Regular

Oscar Mayer -
- Deli Fresh Meats (Shaved Slow Roasted Roast Beef)

Spartan Brand - Corned Beef Hash

Beef Jerky... **see Jerky/Beef Sticks**

Beef Sticks... **see Jerky/Beef Sticks**

Beer

American

Anheuser-Busch - Redbridge Beer

Bard's Tale Beer - Dragon's Gold Gluten Free Lager

Lakefront Brewery - New Grist Beer

Old Hat Brewery - Bees Knees

Ramapo Valley Brewery - Passover Honey Lager

Imported

Bi-Aglut - Special 76 Lager (Italy)

Brauerei Griekirchen AG - Beer Up Glutenfrei Pale Ale (Austria)

Carlsberg Brewery - Saxon Premium Lager (Finland)

Fine Ale Club - Against The Grain (England)

Glutaner - Glutenfrei Pils (Belgium)

Green's - (England)

Discovery

Explorer

Herald

Pioneer

Trailblazer

Hambleton - GFB, GFL (England)

Hambleton's Ale - Pale Ale (England)

Koff - Lager, Taytolainen Keyytolut (Finland)

Laitilan - Kukko Pils III Lager, Kukko Tumma III Dark Lager (Finland)

Les Bieres de la Nouvelle France - La Messagere Pale Ale (Canada)

Liebhart's Privatbrauerai - (Germany)

Bio-Reis-Gold

Bio-Reis-Gold Dunkel

O'Brien - Bown Ale, Pale Ale, Premium Lager (Australia)

Schnitzer Brau - Glutenfrei Bier (Germany)
Silly Yaks - Aztec Gold (Australia)

Beets... **All **Fresh** Beets Are **Gluten/Casein/Soy -Free***

365 Every Day Value - Sliced
Baxters -
Beetroot Pickle
Rosebut Beetroot
Del Monte - All Varieties
Hy-Vee - Fancy (Diced, Sliced)
Meijer Brand -
Harvard Sweet Sour
Sliced (No Salt, Pickled, Regular)
Whole (Medium, Pickled)
Publix - Canned
S&W - All Varieties
Spartan Brand - Diced, Sliced, Whole
Trader Joe's - Steamed
Wegmans Brand -
Harvard
Sliced
No Salt
Pickled
Regular
Whole
Pickled
Regular

Berries... **All **Fresh** Berries Are **Gluten/Casein/Soy -Free***

Cascadian Farm - Organic Frozen Harvest Berries
Del Monte -
Canned Fruit (All Varieties)
Fruit Snack Cups (All Metal & Plastic Containers)

Great Value Brand (Wal-Mart) - Frozen
Meijer Brand -
Frozen Berry Medley
Frozen Triple Berry Blend
Publix - Frozen Mixed Berries
Spartan Brand - Frozen Berry Medley
Woodstock Farms - Organic Frozen Mixed Berries

Beverages... see Drinks/Juice

Biscotti
Orgran -
Amaretti
Classic Chocolate
Lemon Poppyseed

Biscuits
123 Gluten Free - Southern Glory Biscuits
Bob's Red Mill - Gluten Free Wheat Free Biscuit & Baking Mix
Cause You're Special - Hearty Gluten Free Biscuit Mix
Glutano - Biscuits (Shortcake Ring)
Really Great Food - Old Time Biscuit
Schar - Frollini, Milly Friends, Savoiardi

Bittermelon... **All* ***Fresh*** *Bittermelon Is* ***Gluten/Casein/Soy -Free***

Black Eyed Peas... see Peas

Blackberries... **All* ***Fresh*** *Blackberries Are* ***Gluten/Casein/Soy -Free***
Cascadian Farm - Organic Frozen Blackberries
Great Value Brand (Wal-Mart) - Frozen
Meijer Brand - Frozen
Publix - Frozen
Spartan Brand - Frozen
Trader Joe's - Plain Frozen
Wegmans Brand
Woodstock Farms - Organic Frozen Blackberries

B

Blueberries... **All **Fresh** Blueberries Are **Gluten/Casein/Soy -Free***

- **Cascadian Farm** - Organic Frozen Blueberries
- **Great Value Brand (Wal-Mart)** - Frozen
- **Hy-Vee** - Frozen
- **Meijer Brand** - Frozen (Organic, Regular)
- **Publix** - Frozen
- **Spartan Brand** - Frozen
- **Trader Joe's** - Plain Frozen
- **Wegmans Brand**
- **Woodstock Farms** - Organic Frozen Wild Blueberries

Bok Choy... **All **Fresh** Bok Choy Is **Gluten/Casein/Soy -Free***

Bologna

- **Applegate Farms** - Turkey
- **Honeysuckle White** - Turkey
- **Hy-Vee** - German Brand
- **Perdue** - Deli Turkey
- **Shelton's** - Uncured (Chicken, Turkey)

Bouillon/Bouillon Cubes

- **Celifibr** -
  - Bouillon Cubes
    - Vegetable Medley
    - Vegetarian Beef
    - Vegetarian Chicken
- **Harvest Sun** -
  - Organic Bouillon Cubes
    - Chicken
    - Herbal
    - Low Sodium
    - Mushroom
    - Onion
    - Vegetable
    - Yeast Free Vegetable

Kum Chun - Chicken Bouillon Powder

Spartan Brand - Soup Chicken Bouillon (Granular)

Bourbon... **All **Distilled** Alcohol Is **Gluten/Casein/Soy-Free*** [2]

Bran

El Peto - Rice

Kinnikinnick - Rice

Bratwurst... see Sausage

Bread... (includes Rolls)

123 Gluten Free - Aaron's Favorite Rolls

Celiac Specialties -

Mock Rye

Multigrain

Navy Bean

Flaxseed

Regular

El Peto -

Bread

Flax Seed Loaf

Millet

Multi Grain

Potato

Raisin

Tapioca

White Rice

Dinner Rolls

Multi-Grain

Raisin

White

Ener-G -

Sliced Breads

Brown Rice

[2] www.celiac.com

B

Cinnamon Rolls
Corn
Egg Free Raisin
Four Flour
Hi Fiber
Light
Brown Rice
Tapioca
White Rice
White Rice Flax
Papas
Raisin Loaf w/Eggs
Rice Starch
Seattle Brown
Tapioca Loaf
Dinner Rolls
Regular Sliced
Thin Sliced
White (Regular, Rice Flax)
Yeast Free
Brown Rice
Sweet
White Rice
Specialty Breads
Bread Crumbs
Broken Melba Toast
Communion Wafers
Plain Croutons

Food For Life -

Almond Rice
Bhutanese Red Rice
Brown Rice

Fruit & Seed Medley
Multi Grain
White Rice

Glutano -
Cracker Bread
Wholemeal Sliced Bread

Kinnikinnick -
Brown Sandwich
Candida Yeast Free Multigrain Rice
Cubes
Festive
Many Wonder Multigrain Rice
Robins Honey Brown Rice
Sunflower Flax Rice
Tapioca Rice
Italian White Rice
Raisin
Regular
Yeast Free
Tru Fibre Multigrain Rice
White Sandwich

Namaste Foods - Bread Mix

Nu-World Foods -
Flatbread Amaranth
Buckwheat
Garbanzo
Sorghum

Trader Joe's -
Gluten Free
Bagels
French Rolls
Ryeless "Rye" Bread

B

Bread Mix... (includes Baking Mix)

Arrowhead Mills - All Purpose Baking Mix

Authentic Foods -

- Cinnamon Bread Mix
- White Bread Homestyle

Bob's Red Mill - Bread Mix (Cinnamon Raisin)

Breads From Anna -

- Bread Mix
  - Banana
  - Cranberry
  - Pumpkin

Chebe -

- Bread Mix
  - All Purpose
  - Cinnamon Roll Ups
  - Focaccia
  - Garlic Onion Breadsticks
  - Pizza Crust

Ener-G -

- Mix
  - Corn
  - Potato
  - Rice

Gifts Of Nature -

- Basic Muffin/Quick Bread Mix
- French Bread/Pizza Crust Mix
- Sandwich White Bread And Roll Mix

Gillian's Foods - All Purpose Baking Mix

Glutano - Bread & Cake Mix

Gluten-Free Essentials -

- All Purpose Baking Mix
- Holiday Gingerbread

Lemon Poppy Seed
Multi Grain
Cinnamon Spice
Meatloaf Starter
Original
Zesty Italian
Gluten-Free Pantry -
French Bread & Pizza Mix
Yankee Cornbread Mix
Kinnikinnick -
Candida Yeast Free Rice
Tapioca Rice
White Rice
Miss Roben's -
Bagel Mix
Biscuit Mix
Bread Mix
Dinner
French
Homestyle
Noah's
Potato
White Sandwich
English Muffin
Traditional Cornbread
Namaste Foods - All Varieties
Orgran - Bread Mix (Easy Bake, Wholemeal)
Pamela's Products - Amazing Bread Mix
Really Great Foods -
Biscuit Loaf
Bread Mix

B

Brown Rice
Dark European
French
Irish Soda
Old Fashioned Cinnamon
Rye Style
White
Cornbread Muffin Mix
Home Style Cornbread
Old Time Biscuit
Spinach & Cheese
Schar - Classic White Bread Mix
Breadcrumbs... see Coating
Breadsticks
Chebe - Garlic & Onion Breadsticks Mix
Glutino -
Pizza Breadsticks
Sesame Breadsticks
Breakfast
Dietz & Watson - Breakfast Ham Filets
Honeysuckle White - Breakfast Sausage (Links, Patties)
Johnsonville -
Breakfast Sausage & Patties
Home Style
Original
Vermont Maple Syrup
Shelton's - Turkey Breakfast (Sausage, Strips)
Broccoli... **All **Fresh** Broccoli Is **Gluten/Casein/Soy -Free***
365 Every Day Value - Frozen Florets
365 Organic Every Day Value - Frozen Florets
Birds Eye - All Plain Frozen Broccoli ***(Except With Sauce)***

Cascadian Farm -
Organic Frozen
Broccoli Cuts
Broccoli Florets
Freshlike - Plain Frozen Broccoli ***(Except Pasta Combos & Seasoned Blends)***
Great Value Brand (Wal-Mart) -
Frozen
Broccoli & Cauliflower
Broccoli Florets
Cut Broccoli
Green Giant - Frozen Chopped
Hy-Vee - Frozen (Chopped, Cuts, Florets)
Meijer Brand - Frozen (Chopped, Cuts, Spears)
Midwest Country Fare - Frozen (Chopped, Cut)
Pictsweet - Plain Broccoli (Frozen)
Publix - Frozen (Chopped, Cuts, Spears)
Spartan Brand - Cuts, Florets, Spears, Sprouts
Sunny Select - Canned, Frozen
Trader Joe's - Plain Frozen
Wegmans Brand -
Broccoli (Chopped, Cuts)
Broccoli Cuts & Cauliflower Florets
Spears
Woodstock Farms - Organic Frozen Broccoli Florets

Broth

Baxters - Chicken
College Inn Broth - Garden Vegetable
Great Value Brand (Wal-Mart) -
Beef ***(Box Only, Not Canned)***
Chicken ***(Box Only, Not Canned)***

Health Valley -
- Fat Free
  - Beef Flavored (No Salt Added)
  - Chicken
  - Vegetable
- Low Fat Chicken
  - No Salt Added
  - Regular

Imagine -
- Organic
  - Beef
    - Low Sodium
    - Regular
  - Free Range Chicken
    - Low Sodium
    - Regular
  - No Chicken
  - Vegetable
    - Low Sodium
    - Regular

Pacific Natural Foods -
- Beef Broth
- Natural Free Range Chicken
- Organic
  - Beef
  - Free Range Chicken
  - Low Sodium (Chicken)
  - Vegetable Broth

Seitenbacher - Vegetable Broth & Seasoning

Shelton's -
- Chicken (Fat Free Low Sodium, Regular)
- Organic (Chicken, Chicken Fat Free Low Sodium)

B

Swanson -
Natural Goodness 33% Less Sodium (All)
Trader Joe's -
Chicken (Low Sodium, Regular)
Organic Hearty Vegetable

Brown Sugar... see Sugar

Brownies/Brownie Mix
1 2 3 Gluten Free - Divinely Decadent Brownies
Bob's Red Mill - Gluten Free Brownie Mix
Cause You're Special - Chocolate Fudge Brownie Mix
Celiac Specialties - Gluten Free Brownie Tray
El Peto - Brownie Mix
Ener-G - Brownies
Foods By George - Brownis
Gifts Of Nature - Chocolate Fudge Brownie Mix
Namaste - Brownie Mix

Brussel Sprouts... **All **Fresh** Brussel Sprouts Are **Gluten/Casein/Soy-Free***
Birds Eye - All Frozen Brussel Sprouts ***(Except With Sauce)***
Hy-Vee - Frozen
Meijer Brand - Frozen
Midwest Country Fare - Frozen
Pictsweet - All Plain Brussel Sprouts (Frozen)
Wegmans Brand - Frozen (Regular)

Buckwheat
Arrowhead Mills
Bob's Red Mill -
Organic Buckwheat
Groats
Kernels (Roasted Kasha)

Buckwheat Bread... see Bread

B

Buckwheat Groats

Arrowhead Mills

Buffalo Wing Sauce... see Wing Sauce

Buffalo Wings... see Chicken

Buns

El Peto -

Hamburger Buns

Millet

Multi Grain

Potato

Tapioca

White

Hot Dog Buns

Italian Style w/Sesame Seeds

Millet

Potato

White

Ener-G -

Hamburger Buns

Brown Rice

Seattle Brown

Tapioca

White Rice

Hot Dog Buns

Seattle Brown

Tapioca

Kinnikinnick -

Tapioca Rice Buns

Cinnamon

Hamburger Buns

Hot Cross

Hot Dog

Multigrain Seed & Fibre
Tray
Schar - Classic Gluten Free Rolls (Hamburger Buns)

Burgers... **All **Fresh** Ground Meat Is **Gluten/Casein/Soy-Free (Non-Marinated, Unseasoned)***

Applegate Farms - Organic (Beef, Turkey)
Great Value Brand (Wal-mart) - 100% Frozen Beef Patties
Honeysuckle White -
Fresh Ground Turkey Patties
Frozen Turkey Burgers
Original Sunshine Burgers -
Barbecue
Garden Herb
Original
South West
Perdue -
Grill Flavor Round Turkey Burger
Savory White Meat Beef & Grill Flavor Round Turkey Burger
Savory White Turkey Burger
Woodfire Grille Homestyle Turkey Burger
Thick
Thin
Rudi's Hemp Foods - Omega Burgers (All Flavors)
Shelton's - Turkey
Wellshire Farms -
All Natural Frozen
Beef Hamburgers
Turkey Burgers

Butter... see also Spread

Purity Farms - Organic Ghee (Clarified Butter)

C C

Cabbage... **All **Fresh** Cabbage Is **Gluten/Casein/Soy -Free***

Cake/Cake Mix

123 Gluten Free -

Delightfully Gratifying Bundt Poundcake

Peri's Perfect Chocolate Bundt Poundcake

Yummy Yellow Cake Mix

Authentic Foods -

Cake Mix

Chocolate

Lemon

Vanilla

Bob's Red Mill - Chocolate Cake Mix

Cause You're Special -

Golden Pound

Moist (Lemon, Yellow)

Rich Chocolate

Celiac Specialties - Angel Food Cake

Cherrybrook Kitchen - Gluten Free Chocolate Cake Mix ***(Box Must Say Gluten-Free)***

Crave - Mama Z's Chocolate Cake

Dr. Schar - Fantasia, Mix Patisserie

Ener-G - Poundcake

Food-Tek Fast & Fresh -

Dairy Free Minute Cake Mix

Chocolate

White Cake

Yellow Cake

Gifts of Nature - Cake Mix (Chocolate, Yellow)

Glutano - Bread & Cake Mix, Marble

Gluten-Free Essentials -
- Mix
  - Extreme Chocolate Cake
  - Holiday Gingerbread
  - Spice Cake and Muffin
  - Yellow Velvet Cake
- Speedy Bake Cake Mix
  - Spice Is Nice Chocolate Mud
  - Yella Vanilla

Gluten-Free Pantry -
- Angel Food Cake Mix
- Coffee Cake Mix
- Decadent Chocolate Cake Mix
- Old Fashioned Cake & Cookie Mix
- Spice Cake & Gingerbread Mix

Hodgson Mill - Multi Purpose Baking Mix

Josef's - Brownie, Jelly Roll, Marble

Kinnikinnick - Angel Food, Chocolate, Fruit, Sponge, White

Miss Roben's -
- Cake Mix
  - Angelfood
  - Carrot
  - Chocolate
  - White
  - Yellow

Namaste Foods - Cake Mix (Chocolate, Spice, Vanilla)

Pamela's Products - Cake Mix (Chocolate, Classic Vanilla)

Really Great Food -
- Cake Mix
  - Aunt Tootsie's Devil's Food
  - Banana Bread

Chocolate
Chocolate Cupcake
Colonial Spice
Ginger Bread
Golden
Grandma's Pound
Lemon Poppy
Orange
Pineapple
Pumpkin Bread
White
Yellow

The Cravings Place -
Cake & Cookie Mix
Cinnamon Crumble Coffeecake Mix
Dutch Chocolate

Calamari... **All **Fresh** Squid Is **Gluten/Casein/Soy -Free***

Candy/Candy Bars

Altoids -
Mints
Cinnamon
Peppermint
Wintergreen

Charms -
Blow Pop Bubblegum ***(NOT Lollipops)***
Fluffy Stuff Cotton Candy

Cry Baby - Candy, Gum Balls

Dots - Crows, Regular, Tropical

Fluffy Stuff - Cotton Candy

Great Value Brand (Wal-Mart) -
Butterscotch Discs

Cinnamon Discs
Fruit Slices
Gummy (Bears, Worms)
Orange Slices
Spearmint Starlight Mints
Starlight Mints

Haribo -

Alphabet Letters
Build A Burger
Centipedes
Clown Fish
Fizzy Cola
Frogs
Fruit Salad
Gold Bears
Grapefruit
Gummi Apples
Happy Cola
Mini Rainbow Frogs
Peaches
Pink Grapefruit
Raspberries
Rattle Snakes
Sour Cherries
Strawberries
Super Cola
Techno Bears
Twin Cherries

Hershey's -

Jolly Ranchers (Hard Candy)

Hy-Vee -
- Butterscotch Buttons
- Cinnamon Imperials
- Circus Peanuts
- Dum Dum Suckers
- Gum Drops
- Gummi (Bears, Sour Squiggles, Squiggles)
- Lemon Drops
- Orange Slices
- Smarties
- Spice Drops
- Starlight Kisses

Jolly Ranchers - Hard Candy

Kroger Brand - Hard Candy

Let's Do... Organic -
- Fruity Gummi Feet
- Gummi Bears
  - Classic
  - Jelly
  - Super Sour

Mars -
- Skittles - All Varieties
- Starburst - All Varieties

Nestle -
- Gobstoppers (Original)
- Runts (Original)
- Sweetarts (Original)

Nik-L-Nip - Wax Bottles

Publix -
- Lollipops
- Peanut Butter Bars
- Smarties Candy

C

Sour Neon Gummi Worms
Spearmint Starlight Mints
Starlight Mints Candy
Razzles - Original, Sour, Tropical
Spangler -
Candy Canes
Cane Classics
Dum Dum Canes
Marshmallow Treats
Saf T Pops
Swirl Saf T Pops
St. Claire's Organics - All Candy, Mints, Sour Tarts
The Ginger People - Ginger Chews
Trader Joe's -
Black Licorice Scottie Dogs
Woodstock -
Organic Gummy Cubs (Vegetarian)
Organic Jelly Pebbles (Vegetarian)

Canned Chicken

Hormel - Breast of Chicken, Chicken
Meijer Brand - Chicken Chunk White
Swanson - Premium Chunk Chicken Breast In Water
Sweet Sue - Premium Chicken Breast
Valley Fresh -
100% Natural
Chicken White & Dark
Premium White

Canned Ham

Great Value Brand (Wal-Mart) - Luncheon Meat, Potted Meat
Hormel - Chunk Meats (Ham)

C

SPAM -
Classic
Less Sodium
Lite
Underwood - Deviled Ham
Canned Salmon... see Fish
Canned Tuna... see Tuna
Canned Turkey
Member's Mark
SPAM - Oven Roasted Turkey
Valley Fresh - 100% Natural Turkey (Premium White)
Canola Oil... see Oil
Capers
Peloponnese - Wild
Carbonated Beverages... see Soda Pop/Carbonated Beverages
Carrots... **All **Fresh** Carrots Are **Gluten/Casein/Soy-Free***
365 Every Day Value - Sliced Carrots
365 Organic Every Day Value - Frozen Peas & Carrots
Birds Eye - All Plain Frozen Carrots ***(Except With Sauce)***
Del Monte - All Varieties
Freshlike - Frozen Plain Carrots ***(Except Pasta Combos and Seasoned Blends)***
Great Value Brand (Wal-Mart) - Canned Sliced Carrots
Hy-Vee -
California
Classic Cut & Peeled Baby
Frozen Crinkle Cut
Sliced
Meijer Brand -
Canned Sliced (No Salt, Regular)
Frozen Carrots (Crinkle Cut, Whole Baby)

Pictsweet - All Plain Carrots (Frozen)
Publix -
Canned (Carrots)
Frozen
Crinkle Cut
Peas & Carrots
Whole Baby
S&W - All Varieties
Spartan Brand -
Crinkle Cut
Peas & Carrots (Sliced, Regular)
Sliced
Whole Baby
Sunny Select - Canned, Frozen
Trader Joe's - Plain Frozen
Wegmans Brand -
Baby
Carrots/Potatoes/Celery & Onions
Crinkle Cut
Sliced Carrots (No Salt Added, Regular)
Whole Style
Cashews... see Nuts
Cauliflower... **All **Fresh** Cauliflower Is **Gluten/Casein/Soy-Free***
Birds Eye - All Plain Frozen Cauliflower ***(Except With Sauce)***
Freshlike - Frozen Plain Cauliflower ***(Except Pasta Combos & Seasoned Blends)***
Great Value Brand (Wal-Mart) -
Frozen
Broccoli & Cauliflower
Cauliflower
Hy-Vee - Frozen Cauliflower Florets

Meijer Brand - Frozen Cauliflower Florets
Midwest Country Fare - Frozen Cauliflower
Pictsweet - All Plain Cauliflower (Frozen)
Publix - Frozen
Spartan Brand - Frozen Florets
Sunny Select - Canned, Frozen
Trader Joe's - Plain Frozen
Wegmans Brand - Florets

Caviar
Romanoff -
Pasteurized
Black Lumpfish
Black Whitefish
Red Lumpfish

Celery... **All **Fresh** Celery Is **Gluten/Casein/Soy-Free***

Celery Salt... see Seasonings

Cereal
Alti Plano Gold -
Chai Almond
Natural
Oaxacan Chocolate
Orange Date
Spiced Apple Raisin
Amy's - Cream of Rice Hot Cereal Bowl
Ancient Harvest Quinoa - Quinoa Flakes
Bakery On Main -
Granola
Apple Raisin Walnut
Cranberry Orange Cashew
Extreme Fruit & Nut
Nutty Maple Cranberry

Barbara's Bakery -
Organic Brown Rice Crisps
Organic Corn Flakes
Beech-Nut Baby Food - Rice Cereal
Bob's Red Mill -
Creamy Brown Rice Farina
Gluten Free Mighty Tasty Hot
Organic Creamy Buckwheat
Earth's Best Organic Baby Food - Whole Grain Rice Cereal
Eat Natural - Breakfast
El Peto -
Corn Flakes (Unsweetened)
Cream of Rice
Apple Cinnamon
Brown
White
Ener-G - Crumbles, Rice Bran
Enjoy Life -
Granola Crunch
Cinnamon
Cranapple
Very Berry
Erewhon -
Aztec Crunchy Corn & Amaranth
Brown Rice Cream
Corn Flakes
Crispy Brown Rice (Regular, w/Mixed Berries)
Rice Twice
General Mills - Rice Chex
Glutano - Breakfast Pops, Corn Flakes
Healthy Valley -
Blue Corn Flakes

Corn Crunch Ems
Rice Crunch Ems
Heartland's Finest -
Flavored Ceros Cereal
Cinnamon
Original
Kinnikinnick - Kinni Crisp Rice Cereal
Lundberg - Hot 'n Creamy Purely Organic Rice
Nabisco - Cream Of Rice Hot Cereal
Nature's Path -
Envirokidz Organic
Amazon Frosted Flakes
Nature's Path Organic
Crispy Rice
New Morning - Cocoa Crispy Rice
Nu World Foods -
Amaranth Berry
Amaranth O's (Original, Peach)
Cereal Snaps (Cinnamon, Cocoa, Original)
Puffed Amaranth Cereal
Perky's -
Apple Cinnamon O's
Frosted O's
Nutty Flax
Nutty Rice
Original O's
Pocono - Cream of Buckwheat
Schar - Solena Corn Flakes
Seitenbacher - Maize Flakes
Spartan Brand - Quick Grits
Trader Joe's -
Gluten Free Granola

Golden Roasted
Flaxseed w/Blueberries
Whole Flaxseed
Wegmans Brand - Fruity Rice Crisps
Chamomile Tea... see Tea
Champagne... **All Champagne **made in USA** is **Gluten/Casein/Soy-Free***
Cheese
Eat In The Raw -
Parma Vegan Parmesan
Cayenne
Chipotle
Original
Galaxy Nutritional Foods -
Rice Vegan Slices
American
Cheddar
Pepper Jack
Road's End Organics -
Gluten Free
Alfredo Chreese Mix
Cheddar Style Chreese Mix
Nacho Chreese Dip (Mild, Spicy)
Cherries... **All **Fresh** Cherries Are **Gluten/Casein/Soy -Free***
Cascadian Farm - Organic Frozen Sweet Cherries
Food Club - Maraschino
Haribo's - Cherries (Sour, Twin)
Hy-Vee -
Frozen Cherry Berry Blend
Green Maraschino Cherries
Red Maraschino Cherries (Regular, w/Stems)

C

Meijer Brand -
- Dark Sweet
- Maraschino Cherry
  - Red
  - Red w/Stems
- Tart

Midwest Country Fare - Maraschino

Publix - Frozen Dark Sweet

S&W - All Varieties

Spartan Brand -
- Cherries Dark Sweet
- Maraschino Cherries
  - Green
  - Red
  - Red w/Stems
  - Salad

Wegmans Brand -
- Maraschino
  - Jumbo w/out Stems
  - w/Stems
  - w/out Stems
- Sweet Frozen

Woodstock Farms -
- Organic Frozen
  - Cherry Berry Blend
  - Dark Sweet Cherries

Chewing Gum

Bazooka - Original

Glee Gum - All

Chick Peas... **see Beans**

Chicken... **All **Fresh** Chicken Is **Gluten/Casein/Soy-Free** (Non-Marinated, Unseasoned)*

Applegate Farms -
Organic
Roasted Chicken Breast
Smoked Chicken Breast

Hillshire Farms - Deli Select Thin Sliced Oven Roasted Chicken Breast

Homestyle Meals -
Bulk Chicken BBQ Cooked
Shredded Chicken In BBQ Sauce

Honeysuckle White - Chicken Breast (Oil Browned)

Ian's - Chicken Patties, Chicken Finger Kids Meal

Meijer Brand - Canned Chicken Chunk White

Oscar Mayer - Shaved Rotisserie Style Chicken

Perdue -
Boneless
Fully Cooked Diced Natural Proportion White/Dark Chicken Meat
Fully Cooked Diced White Meat
Fully Cooked Pulled Natural Proportion White/Dark Chicken
Boneless Roaster (Yellow Roaster)
Breast, Back In
Breast CVP, Boneless
Over Stuffed Roaster
Thigh
Thigh Boneless, Skinless
Wingettes, 1st & 2nd Section
Frozen Cornish Hens w/o Giblets
Cornish Halves

- Grade A
- Refrigerated
  - 8 Piece Cut (Untrimmed, w/o Giblets & Necks)
  - 9 Piece Cut
  - Bone In Chicken Thigh
  - Boneless/Skinless Chicken Breast
  - Breast Quarters
  - Broiler Party Wing Portions
  - Chicken Fryer
    - Split Breast
    - Whole Breast
    - Whole Chicken w/o Giblets
  - Clipped Chicken Tenderloins
  - Drumsticks
  - Giant Broiler Wings
  - Halves
  - Leg Quarters
  - Quarters
  - Random Boneless/Skinless Breast
  - Whole Broiler Legs
- Rotisserie Chicken
  - Whole Broiler w/o Giblets & Necks
    - Barbecue
    - Honey Flavor
    - Italian Style
    - Lemon Pepper
    - Nonmarinated
    - Oven Roasted
- Specialty
  - RTC Foil Wrapped Chicken Breast (Oven Stuffed Roaster)

Slicing Skinless Chicken Breast
Tender Select Roasted Chicken Halves
Unbreaded
Chef Redi RTC Fillet
Chicken Breast Fillet
Savory Chicken Breast Fillet
Wings
Boardwalk Wing Salt'n Vinegar Flavored Glazed Wings
Chicken Wing/QF Snak Wings
Jumbo Pumped Ice Glazed Wings & Drummettes
Wing City Fully Cooked Honey BBQ Glazed Wings

Publix -
All Natural Fresh
Frozen
Boneless Skinless Chicken (Breasts, Cutlets)
Chicken Breast Tenderloins
Chicken Wingettes

S'Better Farms -
Chicken
Ballontine
Fingers
Party Wings
Siciliano
Szechwan

Shelton's -
Free Range
Chicken Thighs
Whole Chicken
Organic
Boneless Breast
Breast

Breast Boneless/Skinless
Whole
Whole Legs
Spartan Brand - Chicken Breast Chunk
Trader Joe's -
BBQ Shredded Chicken
Grilled Chicken Breast (Balsamic & Rosemary, Lemon Pepper)
Grilled Chicken Strips
Just Chicken (Plain)
Roasted
Chicken Broth... see Broth
Chicken Noodle Soup... see Soup
Chicken Wings... see Chicken
Chiles
Great Value Brand (Wal-Mart) -
Fire Roasted Green Chiles Peeled & Diced
Old El Paso -
Green Chiles
Chopped
Whole
Chili
Amy's -
Organic Chili
Black Bean
Medium (Light In Sodium, w/Vegetables)
Dr. McDougall's - Crowd Pleasing Chili Mix
Hormel -
Chili w/Beans
Chunky
Hot
Regular

C

Hy-Vee - Hot Chili w/Beans
Meijer Brand -
Hot Dog Chili Sauce
No Beans Regular
w/Beans Regular
Shelton's -
Free Range
Mild Chicken
Mild Turkey
Spicy Chicken
Spicy Turkey
Spartan Brand - Chili (w/Beans)
Stagg -
Classic
Fiesta Grille
Ranch House Chicken
Steak House

Chili Powder
Dr. McDougall's - Crowd Pleasing Chili Mix
Hy-Vee
McCormick
Meijer Brand
Midwest Country Fare
Spartan Brand
Tone's

Chili Sauce
A Taste of Thai - Sweet Red
Great Value Brand (Wal-Mart) - Chili Sauce
Hy-Vee
Las Palmas - Red
Lee Kum Kee - Sriracha Chili
Loyd Grossman - Tomato & Chili

C

Meijer Brand - Chili
Spartan Brand
Trader Joe's - Sweet
Wegmans Brand

Chips

Baken-Ets - Pork Skins (Fried)
Cape Cod -
Potato
40% Reduced Fat
Old Fashioned Kettle Cooked
Robust Russet
Sea Salt & (Vinegar)
Chi Chi's - Corn Tortilla Chips (Fiesta All Natural (Authentic)
Eat Smart -
Potato Chips (Lightly Salted, Sweet)
Veggie Crisps (Regular)
Eden - Brown Rice
Fritos - Corn Chips (Original, Scoops)
Glenny's - Spud Delites (Sea Salt, Texas BBQ)
Great Value Brand (Wal-Mart) - Corn, Corn Diggers
Herr's -
Potato Chips
Crisp 'N Tasty
Honey BBQ
Ketchup
Lightly Salted
Mesquite BBQ Kettle
No Salt
Old (Bay, Fashioned)
Red Hot
Ripple

Tortilla/Corn Chips
Bite Size Dippers
Regular Corn Chips
Restaurant Style
Kettle Brand -
Organic Potato Chips
Chipotle Chili Barbeque
Lightly Salted
Sea Salt & Black Pepper
Potato Chips
Backyard Barbeque
Classic Barbeque
Death Valley Chipotle
Honey Dijon
Island Jerk
Krinkle Cut Lightly Salted
Lightly Salted
Salt & Fresh Ground Pepper
Sea Salt & Vinegar
Spicy Thai
Unsalted
Tortilla Chips
Black Bean
Blue Corn
Chili Lime
Yellow Corn
Kroger Brand - Plain (Potato, Tortilla)
Lay's -
Potato Chips
Classic
Deli Style Original
Kettle Cooked (Reduced Fat Original)

Light Original
Lightly Salted
Maui Style (Regular)
Natural
Country BBQ Thick Cut
Sea Salt Thick Cut
Wavy Potato Chips
Regular
Lundberg -
Rice Chips
Honey Dijon
Original Sea Salt
Pico de Gallo
Santa Fe Barbecue
Wasabi
Maui Style - Potato Chips (Regular)
Michael Season's -
Kettle Style Reduced Fat
Salted
Sea Salt & Cracked Pepper
Reduced Fat
Lightly Salted
Ripple
Salt & Pepper
Unsalted
O Organics -
Tortilla Chips
Blue w/Flax Seed
Blue w/Sesame
White
Yellow
Pinnacle - Original Potato Chips

Pringles - Fat Free (Original)

Ruffles -

- Potato Chips
  - Natural
    - Reduced Fat
    - Regular
    - Sea Salted
  - Original
    - Light
    - Reduced Fat
    - Regular

Snyders of Hanover -

- Barbeque
- Fire Roasted Salsa
- Original
- Restaurant Style Tortilla
- Ripple
- Smokey BBQ
- White Corn
- Yellow Corn

Spartan Brand -

- Potato (Regular, Ripple)

Tostitos -

- Tortilla Chips
  - Light Restaurant Style
  - Natural Corn Restaurant Style (Blue, Yelow)

Trader Joe's -

- Chips
  - Blue
  - Red Bliss
  - Reduced Guilt
  - Sweet Potato

Vegetable Root
Veggie
Organic Yellow Corn (Rounded)
Tortilla
Blue Corn
Organic
Salted
Veggie Flaxseed
White Corn
Organic
Salted

UTZ -

All Natural Kettle Cooked
Dark Russet
Gourmet Medley
Lightly Salted
Grandma UTZ Kettle Cooked (Barbeque, Plain)
Home Style Kettle Cooked Plain
Kettle Classics
Dark Russet
Plain
Sweet Potato
Mystic Kettle Cooked Chips
Dark Russet
Plain
Regular Chips
Barbeque
No Salt
Plain (Flat, Ripple, Wavy Cut)
Red Hot
Reduced Fat (Regular, Ripple)

Tortilla Chips
Baked
Wegmans Brand -
Kettle (Original)
Krinkle
Organic
Blue Tortilla
Cracked Pepper
Roasted Garlic & Onion
Rosemary & Thyme
Sea Salt
White Tortilla
Yellow Tortilla
Regular
Tortilla 100% White Corn (Round)
Wavy
Wise -
Barbeque Flavored Ridgies
Corn Chips
BBQ Flavored
Corn Chips
Dipsy Doodles
Dipsy Doodles Rippled
Regular
New York Deli
Jalapeno Flavored
Kettle Cooked
Potato Chips
Flat Cut
Lightly Salted
Unsalted

Wise Wavy
Reduced Fat Kettle Chips
Tortilla Chips Bravos!
Restaurant Style
Sweet Pepper
White Round
Wise (Jalapeno Flavored, Kettle Cooked, Wavy)

Chocolate
Ener-G - Chocolate Chips
Enjoy Life - Semi Sweet Chocolate Chips
Dagoba - Chocolate 73%, Concado Bar, Nibs

Chocolate Chips... see Baking Chips and/or Chocolate

Chocolate Dip
Walden Farms -
Chocolate Syrup
No Carb Chocolate Dip

Chocolate Milk... see Milk

Chocolate Syrup... see Syrup

Chole
Tamarind Tree - Alu Chole

Chutney
Baxters -
Albert's Victorian
Cranberry & Caramelized Red Onion
Mango w/Ginger
Spanish Tomato & Black Olive
Spiced Fruit
Tomato w/Red Pepper
Patak's -
Hot Mango
Major Grey

Sweet Mango

Wild Thymes -

Apricot Cranberry Walnut

Caribbean Peach Lime

Mango Papaya

Plum Currant Ginger

Cider/Cider Mix

Doc's Draft - Apple Pear, Raspberry ***(Alcoholic)***

Sonoma Sparkler -

Natural

Peach

Pear

Raspberry

Organic

Apple

Lemonade

Woodchuck - ***(Alcoholic)***

Amber

Dark & Dry

Granny Smith

Pear

Raspberry

Wyder's - ***(Alcoholic)***

Apple

Peach

Pear

Raspberry

Cinnamon

Durkee

McCormick

Spice Islands

C

Sunny Select

Tone's

Clams... **All **Fresh** Clams Are **Gluten/Casein/Soy-Free (Non-Marinated, Unseasoned)***

Bumble Bee -

Chopped

Fancy Smoked

Fancy Whole Baby

Minced

Chicken Of The Sea -

Minced

Premium Whole Baby Clams

Crown Prince -

Natural (Boiled Baby Clams, In Clam Juice)

Regular (Chopped, In Clam Juice, Minced)

Ocean Prince - Chopped

Club Soda... see Soda Pop

Coating

Ener-G - Breadcrumbs

Gillian's Foods -

Breadcrumbs

Cajun Style

Italian Style

Plain

Gluten-Free Essentials - Seasoned Breading & Batter Mix

Gluten-Free Pantry - Crisp & Crumble Topping

Hol Grain - Brown Rice Bread Crumbs

Kinnikinnick - Bread Crumbs, Graham Style Wafer Crumbs

Miss Roben's - Breading Batter Coating Mix

Nu World Foods - Amaranth Bread Crumbs

Orgran - All Purpose Crumbs

Southern Homestyle -

Corn Flake Crumbs
Tortilla Crumbs

Cocktail Mix

Holland House -
Mixers
Margarita
Strawberry Daiquiri
Sweet 'N Sour
Tom Collins
Whiskey Sour Mix

Mr. & Mrs. T's -
Cocktail Mixers
Bloody Mary
Bold & Spicy Bloody Mary
Mai Tai
Margarita
Sea Breeze
Strawberry Daiquiri Margarita
Sweet & Sour
Whiskey Sour

Rose's -
Cocktail Infusions
Grenadine
Lime Juice
Mojito
Sweet 'N Sour
Triple Sec

Cocktail Sauce... **see also Seafood Sauce**

Frontera -
Cocktail & Ceviche Sauce
Cilantro Lime
Tomato Chipotle

C

Trader Joe's - Seafood Cocktail Sauce

Cocoa Mix/Powder

Dagoba -

Authentic Hot Chocolate

Chocolate Syrup

Unsweetened Hot Chocolate

Green & Black - Organic (Cocoa, Hot Chocolate)

Hershey's - Cocoa Brown Can (Regular, Special Dark)

Nestle - Toll House Cocoa

St. Claire's Organics -

Cherry

Cocoa

Ginger

Mandarin

Raspberry

Coconut

Baker's - Coconut (Bags, Cans)

Great Value Brand (Wal-Mart) - Sweetened Flaked Coconut

Hy-Vee - Coconut, Flake Coconut

Let's Do... Organic -

Flakes

Lite (Reduced Fat Shredded)

Shredded

Spartan Brand - Coconut Flakes

Wegmans Brand -

Regular

Sweetened Flaked

Woodstock - Shredded

Coconut Milk

A Taste Of Thai - Coconut Milk (Lite, Regular)

Native Forest - Organic Coconut Milk (Classic, Light)

Thai Kitchen -
  Coconut Milk
    Lite Organic Thailand
    Lite Thailand
    Organic Thailand
    Premium
    Premium Thailand
Trader Joe's - Light

Cod... see Fish
All **Fresh Cod Is **Gluten/Casein/Soy-Free (Non-Marinated, Unseasoned)***

Coffee
Caribou - Iced Coffee
Folger's - All Instant & Roasts
Great Value Brand (Wal-Mart) -
  100% Arabica Premium (Ground Coffee, Instant Coffee)
  100% Colombian Premium Ground Coffee (Naturally Decaf, Regular)
  French Roast - 100% Arabica Premium Ground Coffee
  Naturally Decaf Premium Instant Coffee
Hy-Vee -
  100% Colombian
  Breakfast Blend
  Coffee (Instant, Regular)
  Decaf (Instant, Regular)
  French Roast
Kroger Brand - Unflavored (Ground, Instant, Whole)
Maxwell House -
  Coffee Bags (Decaf, Regular)
  Filter Packs & Singles (Naturally Decaf, Regular)
  Instant (Decaf, Reduced Caffeine/Lite, Regular)

C

Meijer Brand -
- Decaf
- French Roast
- Ground
  - Colombian
  - French Roast
  - Lite 50% Decaf
- Regular

Millstone - All Flavors
Mountain Blend - Instant
Nescafe - Taster's Choice Instant (Flavored)
Safeway Brand - Decaf Classic Roast
Sanka - Instant (Regular)
Spartan Brand -
- Coffee (French Roast, Instant, Instant Decaf, Regular)
- Coffee Ground (Colombian, Decaf, Light, Regular)

Trader Joe's - All Coffee
Wegmans Brand -
- 100 % Colombian Whole Bean Medium Roast (Decaf)
- French Roast
- Ground
  - 100% Colombian
  - 100% Colombian Medium Roast
  - Caffeine Lite
  - Decaf
  - Espresso Dark Roast
  - French Roast
  - Traditional
  - Traditional Light Roast
- Instant
- Traditional Coffee Singles

Yuban -

Instant (Decaf, Reduced Caffeine/Lite, Regular)

Roast & Ground (Decaf, Reduced Caffeine/Lite, Regular)

Coffee Beans... see Coffee

Coffee Creamer... see Creamer

Coffee Syrup -

Nescafe - Ice Java Coffee Syrup (All Flavors)

Cold Cuts... see Deli Meat

Collards... see Greens

Communion Wafers

Ener-G - Communion Wafers

Concentrate... see Drinks/Juice

Cookie Mix... see also Cookies/Cookie Dough

123 Gluten Free -

Chewy Chiless Scrumdelicious Cookie Mix

Lindsay's Lipsmackin' Roll Out & Cut Sugar Cookies

Cause You're Special - Classic Sugar

Cherrybrook Kitchen - Gluten Free Sugar Cookie Mix ***(Box Must Say Gluten-Free)***

Gifts Of Nature - Fancy, Triple Treat

Gluten-Free Pantry - Cookie & Cake Mix (Old Fashioned)

Namaste - Cookies

Really Great Foods -

Butter

Biscotti (Anise, Lemon Poppy)

Chocolate Crinkle

Cinnamon

Coconut Macaroon

Versatile

The Cravings Place - Peanut Butter, Raisin Spice

C

Cookies/Cookie Dough

Arico -

Almond Cranberry
Lemon Ginger
Peanut Butter
Triple Berry

El Peto -

Almond Shortbread
Carob Chip
Chocolate (Chip, Coconut)
Cinnamon/Hazelnut
Coconut Macaroons
Gingersnaps
Hazelnut/Raspberry
Old Fashion Sugar

Ener-G -

Chocolate
- Chip Biscotti
- Chip Potato
- Regular
- Sandwich
- Vanilla Cream

Cinnamon
Ginger
Vanilla
- Cream
- Lemon Cream
- Regular

Enjoy Life -

Chewy Chocolate Chip
Double Chocolate Brownie
Gingerbread Spice

Happy Apple
Lively Lemon
No Oats "Oatmeal"
Snickerdoodle

French Meadow Bakery - All Natural Gluten-Free Chocolate Chip Cookie Dough

Gluten-Free Essentials - Vanilla Sugar Cookies

Glutano - Short Cake Ring, Wizards

Jennies - Macaroons (Chocolate, Coconut)

Jo-Sef -

Chocolate Chip (Pecan, Regular)
Cinnamon
Lemon
Linzer
Orange
Sugar
Vanilla

Kinnikinnick -

Almond Biscotti (Regular)
Ginger Snap
Lemon Cranberry

Kookie Karma - All Varieties

Namaste Foods - Cookie Mix

Nana's -

Cookie Bars
- Berry Vanilla
- Chocolate Munch
- Nana Banana

No Gluten Cookie
- Chocolate
- Chocolate Crunch
- Ginger

C

Lemon

Orgran -

Amaretti Biscotti

Classic Chocolate (Biscotti, Cookie)

Lemon Poppyseed Biscotti

Outback Animals (Chocolate, Vanilla)

Pamela's Products -

Ginger (Mini Snapz, w/Sliced Almonds)

Organic Spicy Ginger w/Crystallized Ginger

Peanut Butter

Schar - Frollini, Savoiardi

Trader Joe's - Meringues (All Varieties)

Cooking Spray

Publix - Grill Cooking Spray

Cooking Wine

Eden - Rice Mirin

Holland House -

Balsamic Vinegar

Marsala

Red

Red Wine Vinegar

Sherry

White

Regina - All Varieties

Corn... **All **Fresh** Corn Is **Gluten/Casein/Soy-Free***

365 Every Day Value -

Canned Whole Kernel Corn (No Salt Added)

Frozen Cut Corn

365 Organic Every Day Value -

Canned Whole Kernel Corn

Frozen Super Sweet Corn (Regular, White)

Birds Eye - All Frozen Plain Corn

Cascadian Farm -
Organic Frozen
Super Sweet Corn
Sweet Corn
Del Monte - All Varieties
Freshlike - All Frozen Plain Corn
Great Value Brand (Wal-Mart) -
Canned
Cream Style Corn
Golden Sweet Whole Kernel Corn
No Salt Added Golden Sweet Whole Kernel Corn
Green Giant -
Frozen Nibblers Corn On The Cob
Frozen Niblets Corn (No Sauce)
Hy-Vee -
Corn On The Cob (Mini, Regular)
Cream Style (Golden Corn)
Frozen Cut Golden Corn
Whole Kernel (Gold Corn, White Sweet Corn)
Meijer Brand -
Canned
Cream Style
Golden Sweet Organic
Whole Kernel
Crisp & Sweet
Golden
Golden No Salt
White
Frozen
Corn Cob Mini Ear
Corn On Cob
Whole Kernel

Whole Kernel Golden

Midwest Country Fare -

Cream Style

Frozen Cut

Whole Kernel

Publix -

Canned

Cream Style Golden

Golden Sweet

Whole Kernel Crispy

Frozen (Corn On Cob, Cut)

Organic Canned (Whole Kernel)

S&W - All Varieties

Safeway Brand - Cream Style, No Salt Whole Kernel

Spartan Brand -

Baby Corn Blend

Canned

Corn On Cob

Mini Ear Corn Cob

White Super Sweet Corn

Sunny Select - Canned (Frozen, No Salt, Regular)

Wegmans Brand -

Canned

Bread & Butter

Creamed

Crisp 'n Sweet Whole Kernel

Whole Kernel (No Salt, Regular)

Frozen

Bread & Butter Sweet Whole Kernel

On The Cob

Whole Kernel (No Salt, Regular)

Woodstock Farms -

Organic Frozen Cut Corn
Regular
Supersweet (Regular, White)

Corn Dog
Ian's - Popcorn Turkey Corn Dogs
S'Better Farms - Beef Corn Dogs

Corn Oil... see Oil

Corn Starch... see Starch

Corn Syrup... see Syrup

Corn Thins... see Snacks

Cornbread/Cornbread Mix
Bob's Red Mill - Gluten Free Cornbread Mix
Food-Tek Fast & Fresh - Dairy Free Minute Cornbread Mix
Gluten Free Pantry - Yankee Cornbread

Corned Beef... see also Beef
Dietz & Watson - Cooked
Meijer Brand - Hash
Safeway Brand - Hash

Cornflake Crumbs... see Coating

Cornmeal
Arrowhead Mills - Organic Blue, Organic Yellow
El Peto - Corn
Kinnikinnick - Corn

Crabmeat... **All **Fresh** Crabmeat Is **Gluten/Casein/Soy-Free (Non-Marinated, Unseasoned)***
Bumble Bee - Crabmeat (Lump, Pink, White)
Chicken Of The Sea - White Crab
Crown Prince -
Natural Fancy White Lump
Regular
Fancy Pink
Fancy White

Lump White

Ocean Prince - Pink

Trader Joe's - Crabmeat

Crackers

Edward and Sons -

Brown Rice Snaps

Onion Garlic

Salsa

Toasted Onion

Unsalted Plain

Unsalted Sesame

Vegetable

Ener-G - Cinnamon, Seattle

Hot Kid Rice Crisps -

Rice Crisps

Baby Mum Mums

Natural

Sesame

Kookie Karma - All Varieties

Mary's Gone Crackers -

Black Pepper

Caraway

Herb

Onion

Original

Real Foods -

Corn Thins

Cracked Pepper & Lemon

Multigrain

Original

Sesame

Rice Thins

Cranberries... **All **Fresh** Cranberries Are **Gluten/Casein/Soy-Free***

Ocean Spray -

Craisins Sweetened Dried Cranberries (Original)

Cranberry Sauce

Baxters - Cranberry Sauce

Hy-Vee - Jellied, Whole Berry

Ocean Spray - Jellied, Whole Berry

S&W - Jellied, Whole Berry

Spartan Brand - Jellied, Whole Berry

Wegmans Brand - Jellied, Whole Berry

Crisps

Herr's - Veggie Crisps

Michael Season's -

Lite Baked Potato Crisps

BBQ

Lightly Salted

Snyder's Of Hanover - Eat Smart (Veggie)

Croutons

Ener-G - Plain

Gluten-Free Pantry - Olive Oil & Garlic

Cucumbers... **All **Fresh** Cucumbers Are **Gluten/Casein/Soy-Free***

Curry Paste

A Taste of Thai -

Curry Paste

Green

Panang

Red

Yellow

Patak's -

Curry Paste

Madras

Mild Curry

Tandoori
Tikka Masala
Thai Kitchen - Curry Paste (Green, Red)

Curry Powder
Durkee
Tones

D

Dark Chocolate... see Chocolate

Deli Meat
Great Value Brand (Wal-Mart) -
97% Fat Free
Baked Ham Water Added
Cooked Ham
Honey Ham Water Added
Fat Free
Smoked Turkey Breast
Turkey Breast
Thinly Sliced
Roast Beef
Smoked Ham
Smoked Honey Ham
Smoked Turkey Breast
Hebrew National -
Deli Carved
1st Cut Brisket Corned Beef
1st Cut Pastrami
From The Deli Counter
Corned Beef
Pastrami

Hillshire Farms -

Deli Select
- Baked Ham
- Honey Ham
- Honey Roasted Turkey Breast
- Oven Roasted Turkey Breast

Deli Select Premium Hearty Slices
- Honey Ham
- Honey Roasted Turkey Breast
- Oven Roasted Turkey Breast
- Virginia Brand Baked Ham

Deli Select Sandwich Variety Packs
- Club
- Ham
- Sub
- Turkey & Chicken

Deli Select Thin Sliced
- Brown Sugar Baked Ham
- Corn Beef
- Mesquite Smoked Turkey Breast
- Oven Roasted (Chicken Breast)
- Pastrami
- Smoked (Chicken Breast, Ham, Turkey Breast)

Deli Select Ultra Thin
- Brown Sugar Baked Ham
- Honey (Ham, Roasted Turkey Breast)
- Mesquite Smoked Turkey Breast
- Oven Roasted Turkey Breast
- Pastrami
- Roast Beef
- Rotisserie Seasoned Chicken Breast
- Smoked Ham

Honeysuckle White -
- Chicken Breast (BBQ, Oil Browned)
- Hickory Smoked Cooked Turkey Salami
- Turkey Bologna
- Turkey Breast
  - Cajun Style Hickory Smoked
  - Golden Roasted
  - Hickory Smoked Peppered Turkey Breast
  - Hickory Smoked Turkey Breast
  - Hickory Smoked Turkey Ham
  - Hickory Smoked Turkey Pastrami
  - Honey Mesquite
  - Oil Browned
  - Oven Prepared
- Turkey Breast Estate Recipe
  - Buffalo Style
  - Canadian Brand Maple Oven Roasted
  - Dry Roasted
  - Hickory Smoked Honey Pepper
  - Honey Smoked Turkey Breast
  - Mesquite Smoked

Hormel -
- Natural Choice
  - Canadian Bacon
  - Cooked Deli Ham
  - Grilled Chicken Strips
  - Honey Deli (Ham, Turkey)
  - Oven Roasted (Chicken Strips, Deli Turkey)
  - Smoked Deli (Ham, Turkey)

Hy-Vee - Loaf (Old Fashioned, Spiced Luncheon)

Oscar Mayer -
- Deli Fresh Meats

Cooked Ham
Honey Ham
Oven Roasted Turkey Breast
Shaved
Brown Sugar Ham
Honey
Ham
Smoked Turkey Breast
Oven Roasted Turkey Breast
Smoked
Ham
Turkey Breast
Virginia Brand Ham
Smoked
Ham
Smoked Turkey Breast
Turkey 97% Fat Free
Thin Sliced
Brown Sugar Ham
Ham 97% Fat Free
Honey Smoked Turkey Breast
Oven Roasted Turkey Breast
Smoked Ham
Smoked Turkey Breast

Primo Naturale -
Sliced
Coppa Salami
Dried Chorizo
Dried Pepperoni
Hot Chorizo
Original Salami w/Wine

Premium Genoa Salami
Salami w/Black Pepper
Salami w/Herbs
Sopressata

Publix -
Deli Pre Pack Sliced Lunch Meat
Extra Thin Sliced
Honey Ham
Oven Roasted Turkey Breast
Smoked Turkey Breast

Wellshire Farms -
All Natural
Pan Roasted Turkey Breast
Smoked Turkey Breast
Salt Cured Ham Café Slices
Sliced
Beef Pastrami Round
Black Forest Ham
Cooked Salami
Corned Beef Round
Ham Capicola
Mortadella
Old Fashioned Deli Style Beef Bologna
Old Fashioned Deli Style Beef Salami
Top Round Roast Beef
Virginia Brand Ham)

Dill Pickles... see Pickles

Dinner Meals... see Meals

Dip/Dip Mix

Eat Smart - Tres Bean Dip

Fantastic Foods -

Soup & Dip Mix
Garlic Herb
Onion
Onion Mushroom
Vegetable
Frontera - Guacamole Mix
Publix - Black Bean, Green Onion, Guacamole
Road's End Organics -
Gluten Free
Alfredo Chreese Mix
Cheddar Style Chreese Mix
Nacho Chreese Dip (Mild, Spicy)
UTZ -
Mt. Misery Mike's Salsa Dip
Sweet Salsa Dip

Donuts/Doughnuts
Ener-G - Plain Doughnut (Holes, Regular)
Kinnikinnick -
Chocolate Dipped
Cinnamon Sugar
Maple Glazed
Vanilla Glazed

Dressing... **see Salad Dressing**

Dried Fruit
Eden -
Cranberries
Montmorency Dried Tart Cherries
Wild Blueberries
Great Value Brand (Wal-Mart) -
California Sun Dried Raisins (100% Natural)
Pitted Prunes

Hy-Vee -
- Apples
- Apricots
- Cherries
- Cranberries
- Mixed (Berries, Fruit)
- Pineapple

Mrs. May's Naturals - Fruity Chips (Regular, Sugarless)

Sun-Maid -
- Raisins
  - Baking
  - Golden
  - Jumbo
  - Regular
- Zante Currants

Trader Joe's - All Varieties

Wegmans Brand - Dried Plums, Pitted Prunes

Woodstock Farms -
- Apple Rings (Regular, Unsulphured)
- Apricots (Turkish, Unsulphured)
- Banana Chips (Regular, Sweetened)
- Black Mission Figs
- Calmyrna Figs
- Cherries Unsulphured
- Coconut Shredded
- Cranberries Sweetened
- Dates Deglet
- Flame Raisins
- Ginger (Crystallized, Slices Unsulphured)
- Goji Berries
- Kiwi Slices
- Mango (Diced, Slices (Regular, Unsulphured))

Medjool Dates w/Pit
Papaya Spears Unsulphured
Pineapple (Diced, Rings, Unsulphured Slices)
Prunes Pitted
Thompson Raisins

Drink Mix

Meijer -
Lemonade Stix
Orange Free
Orange Light
Raspberry Stix
Strawberry Orange Banana

Nestea - Iced Tea Mix

Spartan Brand -
Cherry
Grape
Lemonade Flavor
Pink Lemonade
Raspberry
Tropical Punch

Wegmans Brand -
Frozen Juice Concentrate Drink Mix
Lemonade Flavor
Pink Lemonade

Drinks/Juice (Non-Carbonated)...(Carbonated Drinks... see Soda Pop)

Campbell's -
All Tomato Juice
All V8 V-Fusion Blends
All V8 Vegetable Juices

Capri Sun - All Flavors

Cascadian Farms -

Organic Frozen Juice Concentrate
Apple
Cranberry
Grape
Lemonade
Orange
Raspberry

Ceres Fruit Juices -
Juice
Apricot
Mango
Papaya
Pomegranate & Lime

Dole - All Fruit Juice

Eden -
Apple Juice
Concentrate (Apple, Cherry)
Montmorency Tart Cherry Juice

Fruit2O - All Varieties

Great Value Brand (Wal-Mart) -
Juice
100% Juice Apple Juice (Juice Boxes)
100% Juice Fruit Punch (Juice Boxes)
Prune Juice
From Concentrate
100% Juice Apple Juice Punch Blend
100% Juice Unsweetened Apple Juice
Fruit Punch
Kiwi Strawberry Punch
Lemon Berry Punch
Light Apple Juice Cocktail

Natural Strength Lemon Juice
Tomato Juice
Unsweetened White Grapefruit Juice
Vegetable Juice
Frozen Juice Concentrate
Country Style Orange Juice Pure Unsweetened
Florida Grapefruit Juice Pure Unsweetened
Fruit Punch
Grape Juice Drink
Limeade
Orange Juice with Calcium
Pink Lemonade
Refrigerated Drinks
Country Style Orange Juice
Fruit Punch
Grape Drink
Orange Juice

Hy-Vee -
100% Juice Blend
Cranberry
Cranberry Apple
Cranberry Raspberry
Frozen Concentrate
Apple
Fruit Punch
Grape Juice Cocktail
Grapefruit Juice
Lemonade, Limeade
Orange (Regular, w/Calcium)
Pink Lemonade
Juice Cocktail From Concentrate
Cranberry

D

Cranberry Apple
Cranberry Grape
Cranberry Raspberry
Cranberry Strawberry
Ruby Red Grapefruit
Juice From Concentrate
100% Apple
100% White Grape
Pineapple
Tomato
Vegetable
Just Juice
Apple
Berry
Cherry
Grape
Punch
Non Concentrate
Country Style Orange
Orange Juice
Orange Juice w/Calcium
Ruby Red Grapefruit
Kroger Brand -
Fruit Juices
Shelf Stable Juices
Vegetable Juice
Lakewood - All Juices (Organic)
Meijer Brand -
100% Juice
Berry
Cherry
Cranberry/Raspberry

Grape
Punch
Cranberry Juice Drink (White)
Frozen Concentrate Juice (Apple, Grape, White Grape)
Fruit Punch Light
Juice
Apple
Apple Natural
Cherry
Grape
Grapefruit
Lemon
Pineapple
Pink Grapefruit
Prune
Ruby Red Grapefruit
Tangerine & Ruby Red
White Grape
White Grapefruit
Juice Cocktail
Cranapple
Cranberry (Light, Regular)
Cranberry Grape (Light, Regular)
Cranberry Raspberry Light
Cranberry Strawberry
Cranberry White Peach
Light Grape Splenda
Ruby Red Grapefruit (Light, Regular)
White Cranberry
White Cranberry Peach
White Cranberry Strawberry

White Grapefruit
Juice Refrigerated Orange (Original)
Juice Refrigerated Orange Premium
Original
Pulp
w/Calcium
Lemon Juice Squeeze Bottle
Orange Reconstituted
Original
Pulp
w/Calcium
Organic Juice
Apple
Concord Grape
Cranberry
Lemonade
Splash
Berry Blend
Strawberry/Kiwi
Tropical Blend
Mott's - Original 100% Apple Juice
Nantucket Nectars - All Varieties
Nestea -
Lemon
Diet
Regular
Sweet
Lemon Sweet (Hot Fill)
Newman's Own -
Gorilla Grape
Juice Cocktail

Grape
Orange Mango
Raspberry Kiwi
Raz Ma Taz Raspberry
Lemonade
Lightly Sweetened
Organic
Pink
Reduced Sugar Pink
Lemonade Iced Tea
Limeade
Orange Mango Tango

O Organics -
Bottle Juices
Apple
Berry Blend
Blueberry Blend
Cranberry Cocktail
Grape
Lemonade

Ocean Spray -
100% Cranberry Juice
Regular
w/Concord Grape
w/Pacific Raspberry
100% Grapefruit Juice
Ruby Red
White
Cranberry Blends
Cran Apple
Cran Cherry

Cran Grape
Cran Raspberry
Diet
Cranberry Grape Spray
Cranberry Spray
Grapefruit Juice Drinks (Ruby Red)
Juice Cocktail (Cranberry Regular)
Light
Cran Raspberry
Cranberry
White Cranberry
White Cranberry
Peach
Regular
Strawberry
Odwalla - All Drinks ***(Except Super Protein Vanilla Al Mondo, Superfood, Soy Smart)***
Pacific Foods -
Beverages
Hazelnut
Lowfat Almond (Chocolate)
Lowfat Rice (Plain, Vanilla)
Organic Unsweetened Almond Beverage
Original
Vanilla
Publix -
From Concentrate
Orange Juice (Regular, w/Calcium)
Refrigerated
Premium Orange Juice
Calcium Plus
Grove Pure

Old Fashioned
Original
Premium Ruby Red Grapefruit Juice
Shelf Stable
Apple
Cranberry (Apple Juice Cocktail, Juice Cocktail)
Grape
Grape Cranberry Juice Cocktail
Pineapple
Raspberry Cranberry Juice Cocktail
Ruby Red Grapefruit
Tomato
White Grape

Safeway Brand -
Juice
Apple (Cider, Regular)
Cranberry
Apple
Cocktail
Grape Cocktail
Light Cocktail
Raspberry
Grapefruit (Regular, Ruby Red Cocktail)
Lemon
Orange
Prune
White Grape

SoBe -
Elixir (Cranberry Grapefruit, Orange Carrot)
Green Tea
Nirvana
Synergy (Fruit, Kiwi Strawberry)

D

Spartan Brand -
- Apple Juice (Natural, Regular)
- Cranberry Drink
  - Apple
  - Grape
  - RaspberryStrawberry
- Cranberry Juice Cocktail
  - Low Calorie
  - Regular
- Frozen Concentrate
  - Apple Juice
  - Grape Juice Cocktail
  - Fruit Punch
  - Grapefruit Juice
  - Lemonade
  - Orange Juice
    - Country Style
    - Pulp Free
    - Regular, w/Calcium
  - Pink Lemonade
- Grape Juice (Regular, White)
- Grapefruit Juice
- Lemon Juice
- Premium Orange Juice
  - Country Style Pulp
  - Regular
  - w/Calcium
- Prune Juice
- Ruby Red Grapefruit Juice
- Tomato Juice
- Vegetable Juice Cocktail

Tang - Regular, Sugar Free
Trader Joe's -
All Juices ***(Except Green Juice Blend (Fresh) and Green Plant (Shelf-Stable))***
French Market Lemonade (All Flavors)
V8 - All Varieties
Vruit -
Apple Carrot
Berry Veggie
Orange Veggie
Walnut Farms -
Apple
Apricot
Blueberry
Cherry
Concord Grape
Cranberry
Cranberry Blueberry
Cranberry Raspberry
Incredible Vegetable
Mango Nectar
Orange Carrot
Peach
Pineapple
Raspberry
Wegmans Brand -
100% Juice
Cranberry (Blend, Raspberry)
Ruby Red Grapefruit Blend
Frozen Juice Concentrate
Drink Mix
Lemonade Flavor

    - Pink Lemonade
  - Lemonade
  - Limeade
  - Orange Juice
    - Country Style
    - Pulp Free
    - w/Calcium
  - Pink Lemonade
- Juice
  - Apple
  - Apple Blend
    - Berry Flavor
    - Grape
    - Raspberry
  - Apple Calcium Fortified
  - Apple Natural
  - Cranberry
    - Peach
    - Raspberry
    - Regular
  - Grape
    - Regular
    - White
  - Juice Blends
    - Blueberry
    - Cherry
    - Concord Grape Cranberry
    - Cranberry (Apple, Regular)
    - Ruby Red Grapefruit
    - White Grape Cranberry
    - White Grape Peach

D

- Lemon Juice Reconstituted
- Orange
- Prune
- White Grape
  - Peach Blend
  - Raspberry Blend
  - Regular
- Juice From Concentrate
  - 100% Juice
    - Orange
    - Tomato
    - Vegetable (No Salt Added, Regular)
  - Blueberry Flavor Juice Blend
  - Lemon
  - Lemonade
  - Limeade
  - Orange Juice
    - Calcium Enriched
    - Regular
    - w/Calcium
  - Pomegranate Flavor Juice Blend
  - Prune
- Organic Juice From Concentrate
  - Apple
  - Apricot Nectar
  - Cranberry
  - Mango Nectar
  - Orange
- Punch (Berry, Fruit)
- Premium 100% Juice
  - Orange
    - Extra Pulp

No Pulp
Some Pulp
w/Calcium
w/Calcium & Vitamins
Ruby Red Grapefruit
Premium Orange Juice (No Pulp, Some Pulp)
Woodstock Farms - Organic Juices (All Varieties)

Duck... **All **Fresh** Meat Is **Gluten/Casein/Soy-Free (Non-Marinated, Unseasoned)***
Shelton's - Duckling

E

Egg Replacer/Substitute
All Whites - 100% Liquid Egg Whites
Better'n Eggs - Original, Plus
Egg Beaters - Original
Ener-G - Egg Replacer
Horizon Organic - 100% Liquid Egg Whites
Hy-Vee - Refrigerated Egg Substitute
Lucerne - Best Of The Egg
Meijer Brand - Refrigerated Egg Substitute
Publix - Egg Stirs

Eggplant... **All **Fresh** Eggplant Is **Gluten/Casein/Soy-Free***

Eggs... **All **Fresh** Eggs Are **Gluten/Casein/Soy-Free***

Enchilada Sauce
Las Palmas - Red

Energy Bars... see Bars

Energy Drinks
Monster -
Assault

Khaos
Lo-Carb (Regular, XXL)
Original
XXL
Red Bull -
Regular
Sugar Free

English Muffins

Ener-G -
Brown Rice English Muffins w/Sweet Potato
English Muffins
Foods By George -
English Muffins
Cinnamon Currant
No-Rye Rye
Original
Kinnikinnick -
Blueberry
Carrot
Chocolate Chip
Tapioca Rice

Extract

365 Organic Every Day Value - Vanilla Extract
Durkee - Vanilla (Imitation, Pure)
Flavorganics -
Almond
Anise
Chocolate
Coconut
Hazelnut
Lemon

E

F

Orange
Peppermint
Rum
Vanilla

Hy-Vee - Imitation Vanilla
Meijer Brand - Imitation Vanilla, Vanilla
Spartan Brand - Vanilla
Sunny Select - Sunnyside Vanilla Extract
Tones - Vanilla (Imitation, Pure)
Trader Joe's - Vanilla (All)
Wegmans Brand - Vanilla Extract

F

Fajita Seasoning Mix... see also Seasonings
Safeway Brand
Falafel Mix
Authentic Foods
Orgran *(New Formula)*
Fettuccini... see Pasta
Fiber
Kinnikinnick -
Easy White Fiber Mix
Pea Hull Fibre
Fish... **All **Fresh** Fish Is **Gluten/Casein/Soy -Free (Non-Marinated, Unseasoned)***
Bumble Bee -
Mackerel
Jack
Salmon
Blueback

Keta
Medium Red
Pink
Prime Fillet (Atlantic)
Red
Skinless & Boneless (Pink)
Tuna
Chunk White
Very Low Sodium In Water
Solid Light Tonno
In Olive Oil
Solid White Albacore In Water
Chicken Of The Sea -
Mackerel
Jack
Salmon
Skinless & Boneless Pink
Traditional (Pink, Red)
Tuna
Chunk Light In Water
Low Sodium
Chunk White Albacore
In Water Low Sodium
Crown Prince -
Kipper Snacks
Mackerel
Jack
Salmon
Pink Fancy Alaskan
Tuna
Solid White In Spring Water (No Salt, Regular)

Great Value Brand (Wal-Mart) - Canned Pink Salmon
Hy-Vee - Canned Alaskan Pink Salmon
Ian's - Lightly Battered Fish
Meijer Brand - Canned Salmon (Pink, Sock Eye Red)
Ocean Prince -
- Kipper Snacks
  - In Mustard
  - Regular

Trader Joe's -
- Marinated Wild White King Salmon Fillets
- Premium Salmon Patties
- Seasoned Mahi Mahi Fillets
- Smoked Salmon

Wegmans Brand -
- Alaskan Halibut
- Atlantic Salmon Fillets (Farm Raised)
- Chilean Sea Bass
- Lobster Tail
- Orange Roughy
- Pacific Cod
- Sockeye Salmon
- Swordfish
- Tilapia Fillets (Farm Raised)
- Yellowfin Tuna (Sashimi Grade)

Whole Catch -
- Frozen Fillet
  - Cod
  - Mahi Mahi
  - Sockeye Salmon
  - Swordfish

Fish Sauce

A Taste Of Thai - Regular

Thai Kitchen - Less Sodium, Regular

Fish Sticks

Ian's - Fish Sticks

Flax Seed

365 Organic Every Day Value - Brown Flax Seed (Bag)

Arrowhead Mills -

Flax Seed Meal

Flax Seeds (Golden, Regular)

Bob's Red Mill -

Flaxseed Meal (Golden, Original)

Organic Flaxseed

Hodgson Mill's -

Milled Flax Seeds

Organic Golden Milled Flax Seed

Travel Flax All Natural Milled Flax Seed

Travel Flax Organic Golden Milled Flax Seed

Nature's Path - Flax (Meal, Seeds)

Spectrum -

Organic Essential Flax Seed

Ground

Roasted

Whole

Trader Joe's -

Golden Roasted

Flax Seed w/Blueberries

Whole

Flax Seed Oil... see Oil

Flour

Arrowhead Mills -

All Purpose Baking Mix

Organic (Buckwheat, Millet, Soy, White Rice)

Authentic Foods -

Almond Meal
Arrowroot
Bette's Flour Blend (Featherlight Rice, Four)
Brown Rice Flour Superfine
Garbanzo
Garfava
Gluten Free Classical Blend
Multi Blend Gluten Free
Potato (Flour, Starch)
Sorghum
Sweet Rice Flour Superfine
Tapioca
White (Corn, Rice Flour Superfine)

Bob's Red Mill -
Almond Meal/Flour
Black Bean
Brown Rice
Fava Bean
Garbanzo Bean
Gluten Free
All Purpose Baking, Garbanzo & Fava
Sweet White Sorghum
Green Pea
Hazelnut Meal/Flour
Millet
Organic (Amaranth, Coconut, Quinoa)
Potato
Sweet White Rice
Tapioca
Teff
White (Bean, Rice)

Dowd & Rogers - Italian Chestnut

El Peto -
All Purpose
Amaranth
Arrowroot
Bean
Brown Rice
Corn
Flax Seed
Garbanzo Fava Bean
Millet
Potato
Quinoa
Sorghum
Sweet Rice
Tapioca Starch
White Rice
Ener-G -
Brown Rice
Gluten Free Gourmet Blend
Potato (Flour, Starch)
Sweet Rice
Tapioca
White Rice
Gifts Of Nature -
All Purpose Flour
Certified GF Oat Flour
Gillian's Foods -
Brown Rice
Chick Pea
Imported Tapioca
Potato (Regular, Starch)
Rice

F

Gluten-Free Pantry -
Beth's All Purpose Gluten Free Baking Flour
Heartland's Finest -
Expandex Modified Tapioca Starch
Navy Bean
Performance Blend
Pinto Bean
Hodgson Mill - Brown Rice, Buckwheat
Kinnikinnick -
All Purpose Celiac
Brown Rice
Corn
Sweet Rice
White Rice
Lotus Foods - Bhutanese Red Rice Flour
Lundberg - Brown Rice Flour (Eco Farmed, Organic)
Montina - All Purpose Baking Flour Blend, Supplement
Nu-World Foods -
Amaranth
Flour
Pre Gel Powder
Toasted Bran Flour
Pocono - Buckwheat
Twin Valley Mills - Sorghum
Food Coloring
Durkee
Hy-Vee - Assorted
Frankfurters... see Sausage
French Fries
Alexia Foods -
Frozen
Hanna Gold Sweet Potato Fries (Julienne)

Olive Oil
Rosemary Garlic Fries
Sea Salt Fries
Tomatoes & Pesto Potatoes
Organic
Classic Oven Crinkles
Oven Crinkle Fries (Salt & Pepper)
Yukon Gold Hash Browns
Oven Crinkles (Onion & Garlic)
Potato Nuggets
Waffle Fries w/Seasoned Salt
Cascadian Farm -
Organic Frozen
Country Style Potatoes
Crinkle Cut French Fries
Hash Browns
Shoe String Fries
Spud Puppies
Straight Cut French Fries
Wedge Cut Oven Fries
Funster - Natural Potato Letters (Original)
Ian's - Alphatots, Supertots
Meijer Brand - Frozen French Fries (Quickie Crinkles)
Ore-Ida - Potatoes O'Brien
Woodstock Farms -
Organic Frozen
Crinkle Cut Oven Fries
Shredded Hash Browns
Tastee Taters

Frosting... see Baking Decorations & Frostings
Frozen Desserts... see Ice Cream
Frozen Dinners... see Meals

F

Frozen Yogurt... see Ice Cream

Fruit Bars... see Bars

Fruit Blend

Woodstock Farms - Organic Frozen Tropical

Fruit Cocktail

Del Monte -

Canned Fruit (All Varieties)

Fruit Snack Cups (All Metal & Plastic Containers)

Great Value Brand (Wal-Mart) -

Fruit Cocktail In Heavy Syrup

Fruit Cocktail Sweetened With Splenda

Hy-Vee - Lite, Regular

Meijer Brand - Heavy Syrup, In Juice, In Pear Juice Lite

Midwest Country Fare - Regular

Spartan Brand - Heavy Syrup, Light Juice

Wegmans Brand - In Heavy Syrup, In Pear Juice, Regular

Fruit Drinks... see Drinks/Juice

Fruit Leather

Stretch Island Fruit Co. - Original Fruit Leathers

Trader Joe's - Fruit Rolls (Strawberry)

Fruit Salad

Meijer Brand - Tropical

Native Forest - Organic Tropical

Fruit Snacks... see also Snacks

Fruit Flavored Snacks -

Care Bears

Cinderella

Looney Tunes

My Little Pony

Polly Pocket

Scooby-Doo

Shark Bites
Spiderman
Teenage Mutant Ninja Turtles
Tonka

Fruit Gushers -
Fruitomic Punch
Rockin' Blue Raspberry
Strawberry Splash
Triple Berry Shock
Triple Berry Shock/Passion Berry Punch
Tropical Flavors
Variety Pack
    Strawberry Splash
    Tropical Flavors
    Watermelon Blast
Watermelon Blast

Fruit Roll-Ups -
Blastin' Berry Hot Colors
Flavor Wave
Strawberry (Regular)
Tropical Tie-Dye
Variety Pack
    Cherry Orange Wildfire
    Strawberry
    Tropical Tie-Dye

Great Value Brand (Wal-Mart) - Fruit Smiles

Meijer Brand -
Fruit Rolls
    Justice League Berry
    Rescue Heroes
    Strawberry (Garfield, Regular)
    Wildberry Rush

Fruit Snacks
Curious George
Justice League (Big Box, Regular)
Mixed Fruit
Peanuts
Rescue Heroes Big Box
Variety Pack (Big Boy, Regular)
Veggie Tales

Fruit Spread... see Jam/Jelly... see Spread

G

Gai Lan... **All **Fresh** Gai Lan Is **Gluten/Casein/Soy-Free***

Garbanzo Beans... see Beans

Garlic... **All **Fresh** Garlic Is **Gluten/Casein/Soy-Free***

Trader Joe's - Crushed

Garlic Powder... see Seasonings

Garlic Salt... see Seasonings

Gelatin

Certo - Premium Liquid Fruit Pectin

Great Value Brand (Wal-Mart) -
Cherry (Regular, Sugar Free)
Lemon (Regular)
Lime (Regular, Sugar Free)
Orange (Regular, Sugar Free)
Peach (Regular, Sugar Free)
Raspberry (Sugar Free)
Strawberry (Regular, Sugar Free)
Strawberry Banana (Sugar Free)

Hy-Vee -
Gelatin

Cherry
Cranberry
Lemon
Lime
Orange
Raspberry
Strawberry
Sugar Free
Cherry
Cranberry
Lime
Orange
Raspberry
Strawberry
Jell-O -
Regular Instant
Berry Blue
Black Cherry
Cherry
Cranberry
Grape
Island Pineapple
Lemon
Lime
Margarita
Orange
Peach
Pina Colada
Pineapple
Raspberry
Strawberry (Banana, Daquiri, Kiwi, Regular)
Watermelon

Wild Strawberry
Sugar Free Low Calorie
Black Cherry
Cherry
Cranberry
Lemon
Lime
Mixed Fruit
Orange
Peach
Raspberry
Strawberry (Banana, Kiwi, Regular)
Sugar Free Low Calorie Snacks
Cherry/Black Cherry
Orange/Lemon Lime
Orange/Raspberry
Peach/Watermelon
Strawberry
Strawberry Kiwi Tropical Berry

Kroger Brand -
Flavored
Plain
Snack Cups

Meijer Brand -
Gelatin Dessert
Berry Blue
Cherry
Cranberry
Grape
Lime
Orange
Raspberry

Strawberry
Unflavored
Wild Strawberry
Sugar Free Gelatin Dessert
Cherry
Cranberry
Lime
Orange
Raspberry
Strawberry

Spartan Brand -
Berry Blue
Cherry (Regular, Sugar Free)
Lime (Regular, Sugar Free)
Orange (Regular, Sugar Free)
Raspberry (Regular, Sugar Free)
Strawberry (Regular, Sugar Free)

Wegmans Brand -
Orange & Raspberry Variety Pack
Strawberry
Sugar Free
Cherry & Black Cherry
Orange & Raspberry
Strawberry

Gin... **All **Distilled** Alcohol Is **Gluten/Casein/Soy-Free*** [2]

Ginger

Lee Kum Kee - Minced Ginger

Ginger Ale... see Soda Pop

Glaze

Daddy Sam's - Salmon Glaze

[2] www.celiac.com

T. Marzetti -
Fruit Glaze
Blueberry
Peach
Strawberry
Sugar Free Strawberry

Grains

Arrowhead Mills - Amaranth, Hulled Millet, Quinoa
Bob's Red Mill -
Organic Amaranth
Quinoa Organic
Teff Whole

Granola

Bakery On Main -
Granola
Apple Raisin Walnut
Cranberry Orange Cashew
Extreme Fruit & Nut
Nutty Maple Cranberry
Rainforest
Celiac Specialties - Granola
Enjoy Life -
Granola Crunch
Cinnamon
Cranapple
Very Berry
Trader Joe's - Gluten Free Granola

Grapefruit... **All **Fresh** Grapefruit Is **Gluten/Casein/Soy-Free***
Meijer Brand - Sections (In Juice, In Syrup)

Grapes... **All **Fresh** Grapes Are **Gluten/Casein/Soy-Free***

Gravy/Gravy Mix

Barkat - Vegetable Gravy

Emeril's - Eggplant & Gaahlic

Full Flavor Foods - Gravy (Chicken, Pork, Turkey)

Maxwell's Kitchen - Gravy Mix (Chicken, Turkey)

Orgran - Vegetarian Gravy Mix *(New Formula)*

Green Beans... see Beans

Green Olives... see Olives

Green Peppers... **All **Fresh** Green Peppers Are **Gluten/Casein/Soy -Free***

Green Tea... see Tea

Greens

Meijer Brand - Canned Chopped (Kale, Mustard, Turnip)

Groats

Arrowhead Mills - Buckwheat

Gifts Of Nature - Certified GF Whole Groats

Pocono - Whole Buckwheat

Ground Beef... see Beef

All **Fresh Meat Is **Gluten/Casein/Soy Free (Non-Marinated, Unseasoned)***

Ground Turkey... see Turkey

All **Fresh Meat Is **Gluten/Casein/Soy Free (Non-Marinated, Unseasoned)***

Jennie-O -

Extra Lean

Lean

Guar Gum

Bob's Red Mill

El Peto

Gluten-Free Essentials

Kinnikinnick

Gum... see Chewing Gum

H H

Ham

Applegate Farms -
- Honey
- Slow Cooked
- Uncured Ham (Black Forest, Organic)

Bar S -
- Black Forest
- Extra Lean
  - Hickory Smoked
  - Honey Cured
- Virginia Brand

Cure 81 -
- Boneless
- Old Fashioned

Dietz & Watson -
- Black Forest
- Breakfast Ham Fillet
- Cajun Style
- Capocolla
- Classic Trimmed & Tied
- Gourmet Lite (Tavern, Virginia)
- Ham Steaks
- Honey (Cured)
- Imported (Honey Cured Tavern, Prosciuttini)
- Pepper
- Premium Imported Cooked
- Rosemary
- Semi Boneless
- Spiral Sliced
- Tavern

Tomato & Basil
Tiffany Boneless
Virginia Baked
Ejay's So. Smokehouse - Black Forest Ham Steak
Hillshire Farms -
Deli Select
Baked Ham
Honey Ham
Deli Select Premium Hearty Slices
Honey Ham
Virginia Brand Baked Ham
Deli Select Sandwich Variety Packs
Deli Select Thin Sliced
Brown Sugar Baked Ham
Smoked Ham
Deli Select Ultra Thin
Brown Sugar Baked Ham
Honey Ham
Smoked Ham
Specialty Spiral Sliced
Bone In Half
Brown Sugar Cured Ham
Honey Cured Ham
Smoked Ham
Bone In Whole
Brown Sugar Cured Ham
Smoked Ham
Traditional Hams
Bone In Half
Brown Sugar Cured Ham
Smoked Ham

H

Bone-In Whole (Smoked Ham)
Brown Sugar Ham Steak

Hormel -
Natural Choice Deli Meat
Honey Ham
Virginia Ham

Hy-Vee -
Deli Thin Slices
Honey
Smoked
Thin Sliced
Ham w/Natural Juices
Honey Ham w/Natural Juices

Isaly's -
Chipped Chopped
Old Fashioned Baked Deli
Smoked Honey Cured

Oscar Mayer - Deli Fresh Meats (Shaved Honey Ham)

Primo Naturale -
Sliced
Coppa Salami
Dried Chorizo
Dried Pepperoni
Hot Chorizo
Original Salami w/Wine
Premium Genoa Salami
Salami w/Black Pepper
Salami w/Herbs
Sopressata

Publix -
Deli Pre Pack Lunch Meat Extra Thin Sliced
Cooked Ham

Honey Ham
Deli Pre Pack Lunch Meat Thin Sliced
Cooked Ham
Honey Ham
SPAM -
Classic
Less Sodium
Lite
Oven Roasted Turkey
Underwood Spreads - Deviled Ham
Wegmans Brand -
Ham w/Natural Juices Thin Sliced
Cooked
Smoked
Smoked Honey
Wellshire Farms -
Black Forest (Boneless Nugget, Deli)
Old Fashioned Boneless (Half, Whole)
Salt Cured Cafe Slices
Semi Boneless Half
Sliced (Capicola, Tavern)
Sunday Breakfast
Virginia Brand (Boneless Steak, Buffet)
Hamburger Buns... see Buns
Hamburgers... see Burgers... **All **Fresh** Meat Is **Gluten/Casein/Soy-Free (Non-Marinated, Unseasoned)***
Hash Browns
Alexia Foods - Yukon Golden Hash Browns
Cascadian Farm - Hash Browns
Hy-Vee - Country Style Hash Brown Potatoes
Ore-Ida -
9 Count

H

Country Style
Southern Style
Publix -
Frozen Hash Browns
Country Style
Southern Style
Safeway Brand -
Country Style
O'Brien
Southern Style
Wegmans Brand -
Frozen Hash Browns
Country Style
O'Brien
Regular
Woodstock Farms - Shredded Hash Browns
Hearts Of Palm... **All **Fresh** Hearts of Palm Are **Gluten/Casein/Soy-Free***
Native Forest - Organic Hearts Of Palm
Herbal Tea... see Tea
Hominy
Hy-Vee - Golden, White
Meijer Brand - White
Safeway Brand - White
Spartan Brand - Gold, White
Sunny Select
Honey
Great Value Brand (Wal-Mart) - Clover Honey
Hy-Vee - Honey, Honey Squeeze Bear
Meijer Brand - Honey, Honey Squeeze Bear
Spartan Brand - Honey Squeeze Bear, Pure Clover
Sunny Select - Honey

Trader Joe's - Honey (All)
Wegmans Brand - 100% Pure Clover, Clover, Orange Blossom, Squeezable Bear

Honey Mustard Sauce... see Mustard

Horseradish Sauce

Baxters
Dietz & Watson - Hot & Creamy, Red
Wegmans Brand - Prepared Horseradish

Hot Chocolate Mix... see Cocoa Mix

Hot Dog Buns... see Buns

Hot Dogs... see Sausage

Hot Sauce

Frank's RedHot -
Chile 'N Lime
Original
Xtra Hot
Frontera -
Hot Sauce
Chipotle
Habanero
Jalapeno
Red Pepper
La Victoria -
Jalapeno
Salsa Brava

Hummus

Athenos -
Hummus
Artichoke & Garlic
Black Olive
Cucumber Dill
Greek Style

Original
Pesto
Roasted Eggplant
Roasted Garlic Red Pepper
Scallion
Spicy Three Pepper
NeoClassic Hummus
Original
Original w/Sesame Seeds & Parsley
Roasted Garlic w/Garlic & Parsley
Roasted Red Pepper w/Red Peppers & Parsley
Fantastic World Foods - Original
Garden Fresh Gourmet -
Mediterranean Hummus
Garlic Lovers
Original
Pine Nuts
Roasted Red Peppers
Spicy Cilantro
Trader Joe's - All Varieties
Tribe Mediterranean Foods -
All Natural Hummus ***(All Except Spicy Chipotle)***
Wild Wood Organics - Mid East & Low Fat Hummus

I

Ice Cream... (includes Frozen Desserts, Frozen Yogurt, Sorbet)
Alpine Ice -
Bolder Berry
Green Tea Verbena
Hibiscus Rose

Mango Passion
Plum Lucky
Chapman's -
Orange Sorbet
Rainbow Sorbet
Raspberry Sorbet
Cold Stone Creamery -
Sorbet
Green Apple Gummy Bear
Lemon
Raspberry
Watermelon
Dreyer's -
Fruit Bars
Grape
Lemonade
Lime
Strawberry
Tangerine
Variety Pack (Lime, Strawberry & Wildberry)
Variety Pack No Sugar Added (Strawberry)
Edy's -
Fruit Bars
Grape
Lemonade
Lime
Strawberry
Tangerine
Variety Pack (Strawberry & Wildberry)
Variety Pack No Sugar Added (Strawberry)
Hood -
Hoodsie Pops (6 Flavor Assortment Twin Pops)

Hy-Vee -
- Assorted Twin Pops

Meijer -
- Juice Stix
- Party Pops
  - No Sugar Added Assorted
  - Orange/Cherry/Grape
  - RB/B/BR
- Red White & Blue Pops
- Twin Pops

Natural Choice -
- Full of Fruit Bars
- Sorbets

Nestle -
- Shrek Swamp (Pops Ice Pops)

Philly Swirl
- Sorbet Philly Swirl Stix
- Sugar Free Swirl Stix
- Swirl (Stix)
- The Original Italian Ice Swirl

Publix -
- Novelties
  - Banana Pops
  - Junior Ice Pops
    - Cherry
    - Grape
    - Orange
    - Red/White/Blue
  - No Sugar Added Ice Pops

Purely Decadent -
- Coconut Milk Pints
  - Chocolate

Coconut
Vanilla Bean
Rice Dream -
Non Dairy Frozen Desserts
Cocoa Marble Fudge
Neapolitan
Orange Vanilla Swirl
Vanilla
Safeway Select - Fruit Bars (All Flavors)
Sweet Nothings - Fudge Bar, Mango Raspberry Bar
Wegmans Brand -
Ice Pops (Twin Stick)
Juice Bars - FYFGA Variety Pack (Lime, Orange, Raspberry)
Lemon Sorbet

Ice Cream Toppings... see also Syrup
Dagoba - Chocolate Syrup
Hershey's - Chocolate Syrup (Lite, Original, w/Calcium)
Maple Grove Farms of Vermont -
Flavored Syrups
Apricot
Blueberry
Boysenberry
Raspberry
Strawberry
Smucker's -
Specialty Ice Cream Toppings
Berry
Special Recipe Triple
Toppings
Marshmallow

Pecan In Syrup
Pineapple
Strawberry
Walnuts In Syrup
Sugar Free Topping
Strawberry
Sundae Syrup
Strawberry

Iced Tea/Iced Tea Mix... see Tea
Icing... see Baking Decorations & Frostings
Instant Coffee... see Coffee
Italian Dressing... see Salad Dressing

J

Jalapenos... **All **Fresh** Jalapenos Are **Gluten/Casein/Soy -Free***
Old El Paso - Slices (Pickled)
Jalfrazi
Seeds of Change - Jalfrezi Sauce
Jam/Jelly
Baxters -
Jelly
Beetroot In Red Currant
Country Berry
Cranberry
Lemon
Mint
Orange Lemon & Grapefruit
Raspberry
Red Currant
Rhubarb & Ginger

Seville Orange
Strawberry
Cascadian Farm -
Organic Fruit Spreads
Apricot
Blackberry
Blueberry
Concord Grape
Raspberry
Strawberry
Hy-Vee -
Jelly
Apple
Blackberry
Cherry
Concord Grape
Grape
Plum
Red Raspberry
Strawberry
Orange Marmalade
Preserves
Apricot
Cherry
Concord Grape
Peach
Red Raspberry
Strawberry
Meijer Brand -
Fruit Spread
Apricot

Blackberry Seedless
Red Raspberry
Strawberry
Jam Grape
Jelly (Apple, Grape)
Preserves
Apricot
Marmalade Orange
Peach
Red Raspberry (Regular, w/Seeds)
Strawberry
O Organics - Preserves
Polaner - All (Jam, Jellies, Preserves)
Safeway Brand - All (Jams, Jellies)
Safeway Select - All (Jams, Jellies)
Smucker's - All (Jams, Jellies, Marmalades, Preserves)
Sunny Select -
Apricot
Apricot & Pinneaple
Blackberry
Grape
Raspberry
Strawberry
Trader Joe's - All Jams, Jellies and Preserves
Welch's - All Jams, Jellies and Preserves
Wegmans Brand -
Jelly
Apple
Blackberry
Cherry
Grape

J

Red (Currant, Raspberry)
Strawberry
Organic Jammin'Fruit Spread (Red Raspberry, Strawberry)
Preserves
Apricot
Blackberry (Seedless)
Cherry
Grape
Orange Marmalade
Peach
Pineapple
Red Raspberry
Strawberry
Sugar Free Triple Fruit Spread
Apricot/Peach/Passion Fruit
Raspberry/Wild Blueberry/Blackberry
Strawberry/Plum/Raspberry
Triple Fruit Spread
Apricot/Peach/Passion Fruit
Blueberry/Cherry/Raspberry
Raspberry/Strawberry/Blackberry
Raspberry/Wild Blueberry/Blackberry
Strawberry/Plum/Raspberry

Jello... see Gelatin

Jerky/Beef Sticks

Applegate Farms - Joy Stick
Oberto - Beef Jerky (Habanero, Peppered)
Old Wisconsin - Snack Sticks (Beef, Pepperoni) *(Beef **Jerky** Is **NOT** Gluten-Free)*
Wellshire Farms - Snack Sticks (Hot n' Spicy Turkey Tom Tom)

J

Juice... see Drinks/Juice

Juice Mix... see Drink Mix

K

K

Kale... **All **Fresh** Kale Is **Gluten/Casein/Soy -Free***

Kasha

- **Shiloh Farms** - Organic

Ketchup

- **365 Organic Every Day Value** - Organic
- **Annie's Naturals** - Organic
- **Heinz** - Regular
- **Hy-Vee** -
  - Regular
  - Squeezable Thick & Rich Tomato
  - Thick & Rich Tomato
- **Meijer Brand** - Regular, Squeeze
- **Muir Glen** - Organic
- **O Organics**
- **Organicville**
- **Publix**
- **Safeway Brand**
- **Spartan Brand**
- **Sunny Select**
- **Trader Joe's** - Organic
- **Wegmans Brand** - Organic
- **Woodstock Farms** - Organic

Kielbasa... see Sausage

Kiwi... **All **Fresh** Kiwi Is **Gluten/Casein/Soy Free***

Kohlrabi... **All **Fresh** Kohlrabi Is **Gluten/Casein/Soy -Free***

Korma

Amy's - Indian Vegetable

Taj Ethnic Gourmet - Vegetable Korma

L

Lamb... **All **Fresh** Meat Is **Gluten/Casein/Soy-Free (Non-Marinated, Unseasoned)***

Lasagna/Lasagne Noodles... see Pasta

Lemonade... see Drinks

Lemons... **All **Fresh** Lemons Are **Gluten/Casein/Soy-Free***

Sunkist

Lentils... see also Beans

Great Value Brand (Wal-Mart) - Dried

Tasty Bite - Bengal

Lettuce... **All **Fresh** Lettuce Is **Gluten/Casein/Soy-Free***

Licorice... see Candy/Candy Bars

Limeade... see Drinks/Juice

Limes... **All **Fresh** Limes Are **Gluten/Casein/Soy-Free***

Sunkist

Lunch Meat... see Deli Meat

M

Macaroni & Cheese

Namaste Foods - Say Cheez

Road's End Organics -

Organic GF Alfredo Mac & Chreese

Organic GF Cheddar Penne & Chreese

M

Macaroons... see Cookies/Cookie Dough

Mackerel... **All **Fresh** Fish Is **Gluten/Casein/Soy -Free (Non-Marinated, Unseasoned)***

Mahi Mahi... **All **Fresh** Fish Is **Gluten/Casein/Soy -Free (Non-Marinated, Unseasoned)***

Mandarin Oranges... **All **Fresh** Mandarin Oranges Are **Gluten/Casein/Soy -Free***

Del Monte -
Canned Fruit (All Varieties)
Fruit Snack Cups (All Metal & Plastic Containers)

Dole - All Canned, Cups ***(Except Parfaits)***, Cups In Gel, Jar in Light Syrup

Hy-Vee -
Light Syrup
Orange Gel
Regular

Meijer Brand - Light Syrup

Publix - In Light Syrup

Trader Joe's - In Light Syrup

Mango... **All **Fresh** Mangos Are **Gluten/Casein/Soy -Free***

Del Monte -
Canned Fruit (All Varieties)
Fruit Snack Cups (All Metal & Plastic Containers)

Meijer Brand - Frozen Mango Chunks, Sliced

Native Forest - Organic Mango Chunks

Woodstock Farms -
Organic Frozen
Mango
Tropical Mango Blend

Maple Syrup... see Syrup

Maraschino Cherries... see Cherries

Margarine... see Spread and/or Butter

Marinades

Drew's All Natural -
- Garlic Italian
- Honey Dijon
- Kalamata Olive & Caper
- Poppy Seed
- Raspberry
- Roasted Garlic & Peppercorn
- Rosemary Balsamic
- Smoked Tomato

Emeril's - Herbed Lemon Pepper

Hendrickson's - Unique Dressing Marinade & Seasoning

Lawry's -
- Baja Chipotle
- Caribbean Jerk
- Havana Garlic & Lime
- Herb & Garlic
- Louisiana Red Pepper
- Mesquite
- Mexican Chile & Lime

McCormick -
- Grill Mates
  - Baja Citrus Marinade
  - Chipotle Pepper Marinade
  - Hickory BBQ Marinade
  - Peppercorn & Garlic Marinade
  - Southwest Marinade

Meijer Brand - Garlic & Herb, Mesquite

Mr. Spice Organic -
- Sauce & Marinade
  - Ginger Stir Fry
  - Honey BBQ

Indian Curry
Sweet & Sour
Tangy Bang
Thai Peanut

Marmalade... see Jam/Jelly

Marshmallow Dip

Marshmallow Fluff - All Varieties
Walden Farms - Calorie Free Marshmallow Dip

Marshmallows

Great Value Brand (Wal-Mart) -
Marshmallow Crème
Marshmallows (Flavored, Miniature, Regular)
Hy-Vee - Colored Miniatures, Miniature, Regular
Kraft - Jet-Puffed (Fun Mallows, Miniature, Regular)
Kroger Brand - Colored, Cream, Large, Miniature
Manischewitz
Marshmallow Fluff - All Varieties
Meijer Brand - Mini, Mini Flavored, Regular
Publix

Mashed Potatoes

Meijer Brand - Instant Mashed Potatoes
Spartan Brand - Instant

Mayonnaise

Spectrum -
Canola

Meals

Amy's -
Kids Meals (Baked Ziti)
Mexican Tamale Pie
Black Bean Tamale Verde
Hormel -
Compleats Microwave 10 oz. Meals

BBQ Beef & Beans
Chicken & Rice
Kid's Kitchen - Beans & Weiners
Tasty Bite -
Bombay Potatoes
Mexican Fiesta
Punjab Eggplant
Spinach Dal & Basmati Rice
Thai Kitchen -
Stir Fry Rice Noodle Meal Kit (Original Pad Thai)
Take Out Boxes
Ginger & Sweet Chili
Original Pad Thai
Thai Basil & Chili
Melon... **All **Fresh** Melon Is **Gluten/Casein/Soy Free***
Woodstock Farms - Organic Frozen Melon Berry Blend
Milk
Amazake -
Almond
Amazing Mango
Banana Appeal
Cool Coconut
Go (Go Green, Hazelnuts)
Oh So Original
Rice Nog
Tiger Chai
Vanilla Pecan Pie
Better Than Milk -
Rice (Original, Vanilla)
Dari-Free Non Dairy Milk Alternative -
Chocolate
Original

Good Karma -
- Organic Ricemilk
  - Chocolate
  - Original
  - Vanilla

Pacific Foods -
- Low Fat Rice Beverage (Plain, Vanilla)

Rice Dream -
- Enriched Rice Drink
  - Organic Original
  - Chocolate
  - Vanilla
- Refrigerated Enriched Rice Drink
  - Original
  - Vanilla
- Shelf Stable Rice Drink
  - Classic (Carob, Vanilla)
  - Enriched (Original, Vanilla)
  - Heartwise (Original, Vanilla)
  - Horchata
  - Original
  - Supreme (Chocolate Chai, Vanilla Hazelnut)

Thai Kitchen -
- Coconut Milk
  - Lite Organic Thailand
  - Lite Thailand
  - Organic Thailand
  - Premium Organic Thailand
  - Premium Thailand

Wegmans Brand - Rice Milk (Original, Vanilla)

Millet

Arrowhead Mills - Hulled Millet, Millet Flour

Bob's Red Mill - Flour, Grits/Meal, Hulled Millet

Mints

Altoids - Mints (Cinnamon, Peppermint, Wintergreen)

Mixed Fruit... **All **Fresh** Mixed Fruit Is **Gluten/Casein/Soy-Free***

Del Monte -

Canned Fruit (All Varieties)

Fruit Snack Cups (All Metal & Plastic Containers)

Dole -

All Canned, Cups ***(Except Parfaits)***, Cups In Gel, Jar In Light Syrup

All Tropical Fruit Cups ***(Except Parfaits)***, Jar in Light Syrup

Great Value Brand (Wal-Mart) -

Canned

Triple Cherry Fruit Mix In Natural Flavored Cherry Light Syrup

Tropical Fruit Salad in Light Syrup & Fruit Juices

Frozen (Berry Medley)

Hy-Vee -

Fruit Cups (Mixed, Tropical)

Mixed Fruit (Lite Chunk, Regular)

Meijer Brand -

Mixed Fruit (Individually Quick Frozen, Regular)

Tropical Fruit Blend (Frozen, Regular)

Publix -

Canned (Lite Chunky Mixed Fruit in Pear Juice)

Frozen (Mixed Berries)

S&W - All Varieties

Spartan Brand - Heavy Syrup

Wegmans Brand -

Fruit Cocktail

In Heavy Syrup
In Pear Juice
Regular

Mixed Vegetables... **All **Fresh** Mixed Vegetables Are **Gluten/Casein/Soy -Free***

365 Every Day Value - Frozen Mixed Vegetables
365 Organic Every Day Value - Frozen (Mixed Vegetables)
Birds Eye - All Frozen Vegetables ***(Except With Sauce)***
Cascadian Farm -
Organic Frozen
California Style Blend
Gardener's Blend Mixed Vegetables
Stir Fry Blend
Chinese
Thai
Del Monte - All Varieties ***(Except Savory Sides Green Bean Casserole)***
Freshlike - Frozen Plain Vegetables ***(Except Pasta Combos and Seasoned Blends)***
Great Value Brand (Wal-Mart) -
Canned (Mixed Vegetables, Vegetable Medley)
Frozen Vegetable Mix (California Style, Italian Style)
Green Giant - Frozen Mixed Vegetables
Hy-Vee -
Canned Mixed Vegetables
Frozen
California (Blend, Mix)
Italian Blend
Mixed Vegetables
Oriental Vegetables
Winter Mix

Meijer Brand -
- Frozen
  - California Style
  - Fiesta
  - Florentine
  - Italian
  - Mexican
  - Organic Mixed Vegetables
  - Oriental
  - Parisian Style
  - Stew Mix
  - Stir Fry

Midwest Country Fare -
- Frozen
  - California Blend
  - Mixed Vegetables

Publix -
- Canned Mixed
- Frozen Blends
  - Alpine
  - California
  - Del Oro
  - Gumbo
  - Italian
  - Japanese
  - Mixed Vegetable
  - Oriental
  - Roma
  - Soup Mix w/Tomatoes

S&W - All Varieties

Spartan Brand - Mixed Vegetables

M

Sunny Select - Canned, Frozen
Wegmans Brand -
Mix (Santa Fe, Southern, Spring)
Mixed Vegetables (Canned, Frozen)
Woodstock Farms - Organic Frozen Mixed Vegetables

Muffins/Muffin Mix

123 Gluten Free - Meredith's Marvelous Muffin/Quickbread
Authentic Foods - Blueberry Muffin Mix
Cause You're Special -
Classic Muffin & Quickbread Mix
Lemon Poppy Seed Muffin Mix
Sweet Corn Muffin Mix
El Peto -
Muffins
Banana (Sugar Free)
Blueberry (Sugar Free)
Carrot (Sugar Free)
Raisin Rice Bran (Sugar Free)
Ener-G -
Brown Rice English Muffins w/Sweet Potato
English Muffins
Foods By George -
Muffins
Cinnamon Currant English
English
Gifts Of Nature -
Basic Muffin/Quick Bread Mix
Cinnamon Spice Muffin Mix
Cranberry Orange Muffin Mix w/Montina
Vanilla Poppyseed Muffin Mix
Gluten-Free Essentials -
Lemon Poppy Seed Bread & Muffin Mix

Spice Cake & Muffin Mix

Gluten-Free Pantry - Muffin & Scone Mix

Hodgson Mill - Apple Cinnamon Muffin Mix

Kinnikinnick -

Blueberry

Carrot

Chocolate Chip

Tapioca Rice English Muffin

Namaste Foods -

Muffin Mix

Sugar Free

Only Oats - Muffin Mix

Really Great Food -

Apple Spice Muffin Mix

Cornbread Muffin Mix

Mushrooms... ***All *Fresh* Mushrooms Are *Gluten/Casein/Soy-Free***

Birds Eye - All Frozen Mushrooms ***(Except With Sauce)***

Eden - Maitake (Dried), Shiitake (Dried Sliced, Dried Whole)

Great Value Brand (Wal-Mart) -

Canned Mushrooms

Pieces & Stems

Sliced

Green Giant -

Canned Mushrooms

Pieces & Stems

Sliced

Whole

Hy-Vee - Sliced, Stems & Pieces

Meijer Brand -

Canned

Sliced

Whole

Canned Stems & Pieces
No Salt
Regular
Midwest Country Fare -
Mushrooms & Stems
No Salt Added
Regular
Pennsylvania Dutchman - Sliced, Stems & Pieces
Safeway Brand - Canned (Button Sliced)
Sunny Select - Canned
Trader Joe's - Marinated w/Garlic
Wegmans Brand - Button, Pieces & Stems, Sliced
Woodstock Farms - Organic Frozen (Mixed, Shiitake)

Mustard

Annie's Naturals -
Organic
Dijon
Honey
Horseradish
Yellow
Bone Suckin'
Di Lusso -
Chipotle
Cranberry Honey
Deli Style
Dijon
Honey Mustard Sweet & Hot
Jalapeno
Dietz & Watson -
Champagne Dill
Cranberry Honey
Jalapeno

Stone Ground
Sweet & Hot
Wasabi
Whole Grain Dijon
Eden - Organic (Brown, Yellow)
French's Mustard -
Classic Yellow
Honey
Honey Dijon
Spicy Brown
Great Value Brand (Wal-Mart) -
Honey
Prepared Dijon
Prepared Mustard
Southwest Spicy & Sweet & Hot Mustard
Spicy Brown
Grey Poupon -
Country Dijon
Deli
Dijon
Harvest Coarse Ground
Hearty Spicy Brown
Guldens
Hellmann's - Deli Brown, Honey
Hy-Vee - Dijon, Honey, Regular, Spicy Brown
Jack Daniel's -
Hickory Smoke
Honey Dijon
Horseradish
Old No.7
Spicy Southwest

Store Ground Dijon
Meijer Brand - Honey Squeeze, Salad Squeeze
Midwest Country Fare - Regular
O Organics - Dijon, Yellow
Publix - Classic Yellow, Deli Style, Dijon, Honey, Spicy Brown
Safeway Brand -
Mustard (Including Stone Ground Horseradish)
Shaw's Brand - Dijon, Honey
Spartan Brand - Dijon, Honey, Sweet & Hot
Trader Joe's - Dijon, Organic Yellow
Wegmans Brand -
Classic Yellow
Dijon (Traditional)
Horseradish
Spicy Brown
Woodstock - Organic (Dijon, Stoneground, Yellow)

N

Noodles... see also Pasta
A Taste of Thai -
Rice Noodles
Regular
Thin
Vermicelli
Wide
Celiac Specialties -
Egg Noodles
Linguini Noodles
Seitenbacher -
Noodles

Golden
Ribbon
Rigatoni
Thai Kitchen -
Rice Noodles
Stir Fry Rice Noodles
Thin Rice Noodles
Stir Fry Rice Noodle Meal Kit (Original Pad Thai)
Take Out Boxes
Ginger & Sweet Chili
Original Pad Thai
Thai Basil & Chili

Nut Butter... see Peanut Butter

Nuts

Frito Lay -
Cashews
Honey Roasted Peanuts
Hy-Vee -
Black Walnuts
English Walnut Pieces
English Walnuts
Natural Almonds (Regular, Sliced)
Pecan (Pieces, Regular)
Raw Spanish Peanuts
Salted Peanuts (Blanched, Spanish)
Slivered Almonds
Meijer Brand -
Almonds
Blanched Sliced
Blanched Slivered
Natural Sliced
Slivered

Whole
Peanuts
Dry Roasted
Lightly Salted
Regular
Unsalted
Pecan (Chips, Halves)
Walnuts
Black
Chips
Halves & Pieces

Nut Harvest -
Natural
Honey Roasted Peanuts
Lightly Roasted Almonds
Sea Salted Peanuts
Sea Salted Whole Cashews

Publix -
Almonds (Naturally Whole, Sliced)
Macadamia
Peanuts Dry Roasted
Lightly Salted
Salted
Unsalted
Pecans (Halves)
Pistachios
Walnuts

Safeway Brand -
Nuts Cashews (Halves, Pieces, Whole)
Roasted/Salted Spanish

Spartan Brand -
Peanuts

Dry Roasted (Regular)
Lightly Salted Dry Roasted
Trader Joe's -
All Raw & Roasted Nuts
Almond Nut Meal
Antioxidant Nut & Berry Mix
Candied Macadamia
Cinnamon Almonds
Marcona Almonds (All)
True North -
Clusters
Almond
Peanut
Pecan Almond Peanut
Wegmans Brand -
Dry Roasted
Macadamias
Seasoned Peanuts
Seasoned Sunflower Kernels
Unsalted Peanuts
Marcona Almonds (Roasted & Salted)
Natural Whole Almonds
Peanuts Dry Roasted (Lightly Salted, Seasoned)
Peanuts
Salted In The Shell
Unsalted In The Shell
Roasted
Virginia Peanuts (Salted)
Woodstock Farms -
Organic Almonds (Non Pareil, Regular)
Brazil

Cashew Large Whole (Regular, Roasted)
Deluxe Mixed Nuts Roasted
Extra Fancy Mixed Nuts
Hazelnut Filberts
Pecan Halves
Pine

O

Oats

Bob's Red Mill -
Gluten Free Rolled Oats
Gluten Free Steel Cut Oats
Gifts of Nature - Certified GF Rolled Oats
Gluten-Free Oats - Old Fashioned Rolled Oats
Lara's - Rolled Oats

Oil

365 Every Day Value -
Expeller Pressed Canola Oil
Extra Virgin Olive Oil (Italian, Regular)
365 Organic Every Day Value -
Expeller Pressed Canola Oil
Olive Oil Imported
Annies Naturals -
Flavored (Basil, Herb (Dipping))
Roasted Garlic (Extra Virgin)
Roasted Pepper
Bionaturae - Organic Extra Virgin Olive Oil
Carapelli - Olive Oil (All Varieties)
Crisco -
100% Pure Extra Virgin Olive

Light Olive
Pure (Canola, Corn, Olive)
Eden -
Olive Oil Spanish Extra Virgin
Organic
Hot Pepper Sesame Oil
Safflower Oil
Sesame Oil Extra Virgin
Toasted Sesame Oil
Great Value Brand (Wal-Mart) -
Olive Oil (Extra Virgin, Light Tasting)
Pure Oil (Canola, Corn)
House of Tsang - Wok Oil
Hy-Vee -
100% Pure Oil (Canola, Corn)
Kroger Brand - Canola, Corn, Olive, Sunflower
Meijer Brand -
Blended Canola
Canola
Corn
Oil Olive
100% Pure Italian Classic
Extra Virgin (Italian Classic, Regular),
Italian Select Premium Extra Virgin
Milder Tasting
Regular
Oil Olive Infused
Garlic & Basil Italian
Roasted Garlic Italian
Spicy Red Pepper Italian

Sunflower, Peanut

Nutiva -

Organic

Extra Virgin Coconut Oil

Hemp Oil

Publix - Oil (Canola, Corn, Olive, Peanut)

Spartan Brand -

Canola

Corn

Olive

Extra Virgin

Regular

Spectrum Organic Products -

Almond

Apricot

Avocado

Canola (High Heat Refined, Refined)

Coconut (Refined, Unrefined)

Corn (Unrefined)

Flaxseed

Grapeseed

Olive (Extra Virgin, Extra Virgin Unrefined, Organic)

Safflower

High Heat Organic Refined

High Heat Refined

Unrefined

Sesame

Unrefined

Toasted Organic Unrefined

Toasted Unrefined

Sunflower (Organic Refined)

Walnut

Sunny Select - Canola, Corn

Trader Joe's - Oils (All)

Wegmans Brand -

100% Pure Olive

Basting

Canola

Corn

Extra Virgin (Black Truffle, Campania Style, Novello Unfiltered, Puglia Style, Regular, Sicilian Lemon, Sicilian Style, Tuscany Style)

Grapeseed

IC (Campania, Tuscany)

Mild Olive

Peanut

Pumpkin Seed

Walnut Oil Pure

Okra... **All **Fresh** Okra Is **Gluten/Casein/Soy-Free***

365 Every Day Value - Cut Okra

Meijer Brand - Chopped, Whole

Pictsweet - All Vegetables (Frozen)

Sunny Select - Frozen

Woodstock Farms - Organic Frozen Cut Okra

Olive Oil... see Oil

Olives

Great Value Brand (Wal-Mart) -

Chopped Ripe

Large Pitted Ripe

Medium Pitted Ripe

Minced Pimento Stuffed (Manzanilla, Queen)

Sliced Ripe

O

Hy-Vee -
- Chopped Ripe
- Large Ripe Black
- Manzanilla Olives
- Medium Ripe Black
- Queen
- Sliced (Ripe Black, Salad)

Kroger Brand -
- Black (Not Stuffed)
- Green (Not Stuffed)
- Green Pimento Stuffed

Meijer Brand -
- Manzanilla Stuffed
  - Placed
  - Thrown
  - Tree
- Queen
  - Stuffed Placed
  - Whole Thrown
- Ripe
  - Large
  - Medium
  - Pitted Jumbo
  - Pitted Small
  - Sliced
- Salad
- Salad Sliced

Midwest Country Fare -
- Large Ripe Black
- Sliced Ripe Black

Peloponnese -
- Amfissa

Atalanti
Country Mix
Cracked Green
Ionian Green
Kalamata
Halved
Pitted
Whole
Publix -
Colossal
Green
Large
Salad Manzanilla
Small
Trader Joe's -
Colossal Olives Stuffed w/
Garlic Cloves
Jalapeño Peppers
Stuffed Queen Sevillano
Wegmans Brand -
Greek Mix
Manzanilla w/Pimento
Pitted Ripe (Colossal, Medium)
Ripe (Sliced, X-Large)
Spanish Salad (Sliced)
Stuffed w/ (Almonds, Garlic, Red Peppers)

Onions... **All **Fresh** Onions Are **Gluten/Casein/Soy -Free***
Meijer Brand - Chopped
Wegmans Brand - Whole Onions In Brine

Orange Juice... **see Drinks/Juice**

Oranges... **All **Fresh** Oranges Are **Gluten/Casein/Soy -Free***
Sunkist

Oysters... **All **Fresh** Oysters Are **Gluten/Casein/Soy-Free (Non-Marinated, Unseasoned)***

Bumble Bee - Smoked, Whole

Crown Prince -

Whole Boiled

Smoked In Cottonseed Oil

Crown Prince Natural -

Smoked In Pure Olive Oil

Whole Boiled In Water

Great Value Brand (Wal-Mart) - Canned Smoked Oysters

Ocean Prince -

Fancy Whole Smoked In Cottonseed Oil

Whole Boiled

P

Pancakes/Pancake Mix & Waffles/Waffle Mix

123 Gluten-Free - Allie's Awesome Buckwheat Pancakes

Arrowhead Mills - Gluten Free Pancake & Waffle Mix

Authentic Foods - Pancake & Baking Mix

Bob's Red Mill - Gluten Free Pancake Mix

Cause You're Special - Hearty Pancake & Waffle Mix

Cherrybrook Kitchen - Gluten Free Pancake Mix ***(Box Must Say Gluten-Free)***

Gluten-Free Essentials - Pancake & Waffle Mix

Grandma Ferdon's - Pancake/Waffle Mix

Hol Grain - Pancake & Waffle Mix

Kinnikinnick -

Waffles

Cinnamon And Brown Sugar Homestyle

Original Homestyle

Miss Roben's - Pancake & Waffle Mix
Namaste - Waffle & Pancake Mix
Orgran - Pancake Mix w/Sorghum

Papaya... **All **Fresh** Papaya Is **Gluten/Casein/Soy-Free***
Woodstock Farms - Organic Frozen Papaya Chunks

Pappadums
Sharwood's - Indian Puppodums (Plain, Spicy)

Paprika... see Seasonings

Pasta
Ancient Harvest -
Elbows
Linguine
Rotelle
Shells
Spaghetti
Vegetable Curls

Aproten -
Anellini
Ditalini
Fettuccini
Fusilli
Penne
Rigatini
Spaghetti
Tagliatelle

Bi-Aglut -
Bucatini
Ditalini
Fusilli
Linguine
Maccheroncini

Penne
Pipe
Spaghetti
Stelline

DeBoles -
Corn Pasta (Elbow Style, Spaghetti)
Rice Pasta
Angel Hair
Fettuccini
Fusilli
Lasagna
Penne
Spaghetti
Spirals

Eden - Bifun, Kuzu, Mung Bean

Ener-G - White Rice (Lasagna, Spaghetti)

Gillian's Foods - Penne, Spaghetti

Glutano -
Animal Shapes
Macaroni
Spaghetti
Spirals
Tagliatelle

Glutino -
Brown Rice
Fusilli
Macaroni
Penne
Spaghetti

Grandma Ferdon's -
Brown Rice

Chow Mein Noodles
Elbows
Fettuccini
Lasagna
Spaghetti
Heartland's Finest -
Elbows
Lasagna
Linguini
Spaghetti
Rotini
Ziti
Lundberg Organic Brown Rice Pasta -
Penne
Rotini
Spaghetti
Mrs. Leepers -
Organic Corn Pasta
Elbows
Rotelli
Spaghetti
Vegetable Radiatore
Organic Rice Pasta
Alphabets
Just For Kids
Penne
Spaghetti
Vegetable Twists
Namaste Foods -
Pasta Pisavera
Taco Shells Pasta

P

Notta Pasta -
- Fettuccine
- Linguine
- Spaghetti

Orgran -
- Buckwheat Spirals
- Buontempo Rice
  - Macaroni
  - Shells
  - Spirals
- Italian Style
  - Amore
  - Rigati
  - Shells
  - Spaghetti
- Low Protein Rigati
- Organic Rice & Corn
  - Fancy Curls
  - Small Spirals
  - Smooth Penne
- Pasta & Sauce Quick Dish
- Rice & Corn
  - Herb Pasta
  - Macaroni
  - Mini Lasagna Sheets
  - Penne
  - Spaghetti Noodles
  - Spirals
  - Tortelli
  - Vegetable
    - Animal Pasta

Corkscrew
Rice & Millet Spirals
Tomato & Basil Corn Pasta
Papadini -
Conchigliette
Linguini
Orzo
Penne
Rotini
Spaghetti
Pastariso -
Organic Brown Rice
Angelhair
Elbows
Fettuccini
Fusilli
Lasagna
Mini Shells
Penne
Shells
Spaghetti
Spirals
Tomato (Penne, Spirals)
Vegetable (Penne, Shells, Spirals)
Vermicelli
Pastato - Elbows, Shells, Spaghetti
Rizopia -
Brown Rice
Elbows
Fettuccine
Fusilli
Lasagne

P

Penne
Shells
Spaghetti
Spirals
Organic Brown Rice
Elbows
Fantasia
Fettuccine
Fusilli
Penne
Spaghetti
Organic Wild Rice
Elbows
Fusilli
Penne
Radiatore
Shells
Spaghetti
Spinach Brown Rice Spaghetti
Vegetable Brown Rice Fusilli
White Rice Spaghetti
Schar -
Anellini
Capelli D'Angelo
Conchigliette
Fusilli
Lasagne
Penne
Pipette
Rigati
Rigatoni
Solena Fusilli

Solena Penne
Spaghetti
Tagliatelle
Seitenbacher - Golden Ribbon, Rigatoni
Tinkyada -
Brown Rice
Elbows
Fettuccini
Fusilli
Grand Shells
Lasagne
Little Dreams
Penne
Shells
Spaghetti
Spirals
Organic Brown Rice
Elbows
Lasagne
Penne
Spaghetti
Spirals
Spinach Brown Rice Spaghetti
Vegetable Brown Rice Spirals
White Rice Spaghetti
Westbrae - Corn Angel Hair Pasta
Pasta Sauce... see Sauces
Pastrami
Dietz & Watson -
Pastrami Brisket
Spiced Beef Pastrami

Hy-Vee - Thin Sliced
Meijer Brand - Sliced Chipped Meat (Corned Beef)

Pate

Kootenay Kitchen -
Vege Pate
Curry
Herb
Jalapeno

Tartex -
Pate
Herb Meadow
Mushroom
Original

Peaches... **All **Fresh** Peaches Are **Gluten/Casein/Soy -Free***

Cascadian Farm - Organic Frozen Sliced Peaches

Del Monte -
Canned Fruit (All Varieties)
Fruit Snack Cups (All Metal & Plastic Containers)

Dole - All Varieties ***(Except Parfaits)***

Hy-Vee -
Diced
Diced Fruit Cups
Halves
Lite (Halves, Slices)
Natural Lite Diced
Peaches in Strawberry Gel
Slices
Yellow Cling Lite Sliced

Great Value Brand (Wal-Mart) -
No Sugar Added Yellow Cling Peach Halves In Pear Juice From Concentrate & Water

No Sugar Added Yellow Cling Sliced Peaches
Yellow Cling Sliced Peaches
Yellow Cling Sliced Peaches In Heavy Syrup

Meijer Brand -
Cling Halves
In Heavy Syrup
In Juice Lite
In Pear Juice Lite
Cling Sliced
In Heavy Syrup
In Juice
In Pear Juice Lite
Frozen
Organic
Sliced
Pallet Mod
Yellow Sliced in Heavy Syrup

Midwest Country Fare -
Lite
Halves
Slices
Slices

Publix -
Canned
Lite Yellow Cling Peaches in Pear Juice Halves & Slices
Yellow Cling Peaches in Heavy Syrup Halves & Slices
Frozen (Peaches Sliced)

S&W - All Varieties

Safeway Brand - Sliced Peaches

Spartan Brand -
Cling Halves
Heavy Syrup

Regular
Diced
Heavy Syrup
Light Syrup
Lite Cling Halves
Regular
Sunny Select - Canned
Wegmans Brand -
Halved
Halved Yellow Cling
Sliced
Sliced In
Heavy Syrup
Juice
Regular
Sliced Yellow Cling
In Heavy Syrup
Raspberry Flavor
Woodstock Farms - Organic Frozen Peach Slices
Peanut Butter
Arrowhead Mills -
Almond Butter (Creamy, Crunchy)
Cashew Butter (Creamy, Crunchy)
Organic Valencia Peanut Butter (Creamy, Crunchy)
Valencia Peanut Butter (Creamy, Crunchy)
Kroger Brand - Natural (Creamy, Crunchy)
Meijer Brand - Creamy, Crunchy, Natural (Creamy, Crunchy)
O Organics - Creamy, Crunchy
Peanut Butter & Co. -
Cinnamon Raisin Swirl
Crunch Time
Mighty Maple

Smooth Operator
The Bee's Knees
The Heat Is On
Santa Cruz -
Organic Dark Roasted
Creamy
Crunchy
Organic Light Roasted
Creamy
Crunchy
Smart Balance - Omega (Chunky, Creamy)
Smucker's -
Goober
Grape
Strawberry
Natural
Chunky
Creamy
Honey
No Salt Added Creamy
Reduced Fat
Organic
Chunky
Creamy
Trader Joe's -
Almond
Cashew
Cashew Macadamia
Sunflower Seed
Wegmans Brand -
Natural Peanut Butter (Creamy, Crunchy)
Organic No Stir (Creamy, Crunchy)

P

Woodstock Farms -

Non Organic Nut Butters

Raw Almond

Tahini

Organic Nut Butters

Almond Butter

Crunchy Unsalted

Smooth Unsalted

Cashew

Classic Peanut Butter

Crunchy Salted

Smooth Salted

Easy Spread Peanut Butter

Crunchy (Salted, Unsalted)

Smooth (Salted, Unsalted)

Peanut Butter

Crunchy (Salted, Unsalted)

Smooth (Salted, Unsalted)

Raw Almond

Tahini

Peanut Sauce

A Taste of Thai - Peanut Satay Sauce

Mr. Spice Organic - Thai Peanut Sauce & Marinade

Peanuts... see Nuts

Pears... **All **Fresh** Pears Are **Gluten/Casein/Soy-Free***

Del Monte -

Canned Fruit (All Varieties)

Fruit Snack Cups (All Metal & Plastic Containers)

Dole - All Cups ***(Except Parfaits)***

Great Value Brand (Wal-Mart) -

Bartlett Pear Halves In Heavy Syrup

Bartlett Sliced Pears In Heavy Syrup

In Pear Juice From Concentrate & Water
No Sugar Added Bartlett
Chunky Mixed Fruits
Fruit Cocktail
Pear Halves)

Hy-Vee -
Bartlett Pears
Halves
Sliced
Lite Pears
Natural Lite Diced Bartlett Pears

Meijer Brand -
Halves
Heavy Syrup
In Juice Lite
Slices
Heavy Syrup
In Juice Lite

Midwest Country Fare - Bartlett Pears Halves In Light Syrup

Publix -
Canned
Bartlett Pears in Heavy Syrup
Halves
Slices
Lite Bartlett Pear Halves in Pear Juice

S&W - All Varieties

Spartan Brand -
Halves
Heavy Syrup
Juice
Lite Syrup

Slices
Heavy Syrup
Juice
Sunny Select - Canned
Trader Joe's - Pear Halves
Wegmans Brand -
Halves
Lite
Regular
Syrup
Sliced
Heavy Syrup
Lite
Regular

Peas... **All* ***Fresh*** *Peas Are* ***Gluten/Casein/Soy -Free***
365 Every Day Value -
Canned
Black Eyed
Sweet No Salt Added
Frozen Green Peas
365 Organic Every Day Value -
Canned Sweet Peas
Frozen
Green Peas
Petite Peas
Sugar Snap Peas
Birds Eye - All Frozen Vegetables ***(Except With Sauce & California Blend Seasoned)***
Cascadian Farms -
Organic Frozen
Garden Peas

Peas & Carrots
Peas & Pearl Onions
Petite Sweet
Sugar Snap Peas
Sweet Peas

Del Monte - All Varieties

Freshlike -
Select (Petite Sweet Peas)
Sweet Peas & Carrots

Great Value Brand (Wal-Mart) -
Canned
No Salt Added Sweet Peas
Sweet Peas
Frozen Sweet Peas

Green Giant -
Canned Sweet Peas (50% Less Sodium, Regular)

Hy-Vee - Black Eyed, Frozen Sweet, Green Split, Sweet

Meijer Brand -
Canned
Blackeye
Peas & Sliced Carrots
Small
Sweet
Sweet No Salt
Sweet Organic
Frozen Peas (Organic Green, Peas & Carrots)

Midwest Country Fare - Frozen Green, Sweet

Publix -
Canned (Small Sweet, Sweet)
Frozen (Green, Petite)

S&W - All Varieties

P

Spartan Brand -
Black Eyed
Green
Peas & Carrots
Sugar Snap
Sweet
w/Snaps
Sunny Select - Black Eyed, Canned, Frozen
Wegmans Brand -
Blackeye
Regular
Small Sweet
Sugar Snap (Frozen)
Sweet (No Salt Added, Regular)
Sweet Petite (Frozen)
w/Pearl Onions
Woodstock Farms -
Organic Frozen
Green Peas
Peas & Carrots
Petite Peas
Sugar Snap

Pepper Rings
Meijer Brand - Banana (Hot, Mild), Hot, Mild
Spartan Brand - Pepper Rings (Hot, Mild)

Pepper Sauce
A Taste Of Thai - Garlic Chili Pepper Sauce

Pepperoni... see Sausage

Peppers... **All **Fresh** Peppers Are **Gluten/Casein/Soy-Free***
B&G -
Giardiniera
Hot Chopped Peppers (Regular, Roasted)

Hot Jalapenos
Hot Pepper Rings
Pepperoncini
Roasted (w/Balsamic Vinegar, w/Oregano & Garlic)
Sweet (Bell, Fried, Pepper Strips, Salad w/Oregano & Garlic)

Birds Eye - All Frozen Vegetables ***(Except With Sauce)***

Hy-Vee -
Diced Green Chilies
Green Salad Pepperoncini
Hot Banana Peppers
Mild Banana Peppers
Sliced Hot Jalapenos
Whole Green Chilies

Meijer Brand - Frozen Green Peppers Chopped

Peloponnese -
Roasted
Florina Whole
Sweet Florina Strips
Spicy Toursi

Trader Joe's -
Artichoke Red Pepper Tapenade
Fire Roasted Red
Red Pepper Spread w/Garlic & Eggplant

Vlasic - Peppers

Wegmans Brand -
Pepper & Onions Mix
Roasted Red Peppers (Whole)

Woodstock Farms - Organic Frozen Tri Colored Peppers

Picante Sauce

Hy-Vee - Hot, Medium, Mild

Pace -
- Hot
- Medium
- Mild
- Organic Picante (Medium, Mild)

Pickled Beets... see Beets

Pickles

B&G -
- Bread & Butter
- Hamburger Dill
- Kosher Dill
  - Baby Gherkins
  - Gherkins
  - Original
- NY Deli Dill
- Pickle In A Pouch
- Sour
- Sweet (Gherkins, Midget, Mixed, Mixed Pickles)
- Tiny Treats
- Unsalted
  - Bread & Butter
  - Kosher Dill
- Zesty Dill

Bubbies - Pure Kosher, Bread & Butter Chips

Dietz & Watson -
- Kosher (Halves, Regular, Spears)
- New Half Sours
- Sour Garlic

Great Value Brand (Wal-Mart) -
- Bread & Butter
- Dill Spears

Garlic Dill Slicers
Hamburger Dill Chips
Kosher Baby Dill
Kosher Dill Spears
Sweet (Gherkin, Pickle Relish)
Whole Sweet

Home Harvest Brand -
Dill Hamburger
Kosher Dill (Pickles, Spears)
Sweet Cucumber Chips

Hy-Vee -
Bread & Butter
Sandwich Slices
Sweet Chunk Pickles
Sweet Slices
Dill (Kosher Sandwich Slices, Relish)
Fresh Pack Kosher Baby Dills
Hamburger Dill Slices
Kosher (Baby Dills, Cocktail Dills, Dill Pickles, Dill Spears)
Polish Dill (Pickles, Spears)
Refrigerated Kosher Dill
Halves
Sandwich Slices
Spears
Whole Pickles
Special Recipe
Baby Dills
Bread & Butter Slices
Hot & Spicy Zingers
Hot & Sweet Zinger Chunks
Jalapeno Baby Dills

Sweet Garden Crunch
Sweet Gherkins
Whole (Sweet)
Zesty (Kosher Dill Spears, Sweet Chunks)
Meijer Brand -
Bread & Butter Chips
Regular
Sandwich Slice
Sugar Free
Dill
Kosher
Baby
Baby Dills
Hamburger Slices
Spears
Whole
Polish
Sandwich Slice
Spears
Regular
Spears (No Garlic)
Whole
Zesty
Sandwich Slice
Spears
Sweet
Gherkin
Midget Whole
Sugar Free
Whole
Midwest Country Fare -
Dill

Hamburger Dill Pickle Slices
Kosher Dill
Whole Sweet

Patak's - Pickles (Brinjal, Chile, Garlic, Hot Lime, Hot Mango)

Publix - All Varieties

Safeway Brand - All Varieties

Spartan Brand -
Bread & Butter Pickle (Slices, Sticks)
Hamburger Dill Slices
Kosher Dill (Baby, Slices, Spears, Whole)
Plain Baby Dills
Polish Dill (Regular, Spears)
Sweet (Fresh, Gherkin Whole, Regular, Slices)

Sunny Select - Kosher Spears, Whole Dill

Trader Joe's - Organic (Kosher Sandwich, Sweet Butter)

Vlasic - All Varieties

Wegmans Brand -
Fresh Pack
Kosher Dill Spears
Polish Dill Spears
Sweet (Bread & Butter Chips, Sandwich Slices)
Whole (Kosher Dills, Polish Dills)
Hamburger Dill Slices
Refrigerated Kosher Dills
Halves
Mini
Sandwich Slices
Spears
Whole
Sweet (Gherkins, Midgets)

P

Woodstock Farms -
Organic Kosher Dill (Baby, Sliced, Whole)
Sweet Bread & Butter

Pie

Amy's - Organic Mexican Tamale Pie
El Peto -
Apple
Blueberry
Cherry
Peach
Strawberry/Rhubarb
Walnut

Pie Crust/Pie Crust Mix

Authentic Foods - Pie Crust Mix
Bread From Anna - Piecrust Mix
Cause You're Special - Homestyle Pie Crust Mix
El Peto - Perfect Pie Dough Mix
Gluten-Free Pantry - Perfect Pie Crust

Pie Filling

Hy-Vee - More Fruit Pie Filling/Topping (Apple, Cherry)
Lucky Leaf - Apple, Blueberry, Cherry, Peach
Meijer Brand - Apple, Blueberry, Cherry (Lite, Regular), Peach
Spartan Brand - Apple, Blueberry, Cherry (Lite, Regular)

Pimentos

Meijer Brand - Pieces, Sliced

Pineapple... **All **Fresh** Pineapple Is **Gluten/Casein/Soy-Free***

Del Monte -
Canned Fruit (All Varieties)
Fruit Snack Cups (All Metal & Plastic Containers)
Dole -
Cups In Gel ***(Except Parfaits)***

In 100% Juice (Chunks, Crushed, Slices, Tidbits)
In Heavy Syrup (Chunks, Crushed, Slices)
In Light Syrup (Chunks)

Great Value Brand (Wal-Mart) -
Pineapple In Unsweetened Pineapple Juice
Crushed
Slices

Hy-Vee -
Chunk
Crushed
In Lime Gel
Sliced
Tidbit Fruit Cup

Meijer Brand -
Chunks (Heavy Syrup, In Juice)
Crushed (Heavy Syrup, In Juice)
Frozen Chunks
Sliced In (Heavy Syrup, Juice)

Midwest Country Fare - Chunks, Crushed, Slices, Tidbits
Publix - Canned (All Styles)
Sunny Select - Canned
Wegmans Brand -
Chunk
Crushed
Sliced (In Heavy Syrup, Regular)
Tidbits

Woodstock Farms - Organic Frozen Chunks

Pistachio Nuts... **see Nuts**

Pizza Crust/Pizza Mix

Authentic Foods - Pizza Crust Mix
Bob's Red Mill - Gluten Free Pizza Crust Mix

P

Cause You're Special - Famous Pizza Crust
Chebe - Pizza Mix
El Peto - Pre Baked (Basil, Millet, White)
Ener-G -
Rice Pizza Shell (6", 10")
Yeast Free Rice Pizza Shell (6", 10")
Food-Tek Fast & Fresh - Dairy Free Minute Pizza Crust Mix
Foods By George - Pizza Crusts
Gifts Of Nature - French Bread/Pizza Crust Mix
Kinnikinnick - Pizza Crust (7", 10")
Namaste - Pizza Crust Mix
Orgran - Pizza & Pastry Mix *(New Formula)*
Pizza Sauce... see also Sauces
Meijer Brand - Regular
Muir Glen - Regular
Trader Joe's - Fat Free
Plum Sauce
Wok Mei - All Natural Plum Sauce
Plums... **All **Fresh** Plums Are **Gluten/Casein/Soy-Free***
Hy-Vee - Purple Plums
Wegmans Brand - Dried Plums
Polenta
Bob's Red Mill - Corn Grits/Polenta
Food Merchants Brand -
Ready Made Organic
Basil & Garlic
Green Chili Cilantro
Sun Dried Tomato & Garlic
Traditional Italian
San Gennaro -
Basil Garlic
Sundried Tomato & Garlic

Traditional Italian
Trader Joe's - Organic Polenta
Pop... see Soda Pop
Popcorn
Eden - Kernels
Farmer Steve's - Kernels, Organic Microwave
Hy-Vee -
Regular (White, Yellow)
Kroger Brand - Plain Popcorn Kernels
Meijer Brand -
Microwave
Kettle Sweet & Salty
Natural Lite
Organic Original
Regular Kernels (White, Yellow)
Newman's Own -
Microwave 100 Calorie Natural (Mini Bags)
Regular (Raw Popcorn)
O Organics - Microwave Popcorn (Organic)
Skeete & Ike's - Sea Salt
Trader Joe's -
Gourmet White
Lite Popcorn 50% Less Salt
Wegmans Brand -
Regular Kernels- Yellow
Pork... **All **Fresh** Pork Is **Gluten/Casein/Soy -Free (Non-Marinated, Unseasoned)***
Dietz & Watson -
Barbecue Roast of Pork
Boneless Pork Chop
Italian Style Roast Pork
Roast Sirloin Of Pork

P

Smoked Pork Shoulder Butts

Homestyle Meals -

Bulk Pork BBQ Cooked

Shredded Pork in BBQ Sauce

Hormel - Pickled (Pigs Feet, Pork Hocks)

Trader Joe's - Refrigerated BBQ Shredded Pork

Wegmans Brand - Pork & Beans In Tomato Sauce (Canned)

Potato Chips... see Chips

Potato Crisps... see Crisps

Potato Puffs... see Snacks

Potatoes... **All **Fresh** Potatoes Are **Gluten/Casein/Soy-Free***

Alexia Foods -

Frozen

Hanna Gold Sweet Potato Fries (Julienne)

Olive Oil (& Rosemary Garlic Fries, & Sea Salt Fries, Tomatoes & Pesto Potatoes)

Organic (Classic Oven Crinkles, Oven Crinkle Fries (Salt & Pepper), Yukon Gold Hash Browns)

Oven Crinkles (Onion & Garlic)

Potato Nuggets

Waffle Fries w/Seasoned Salt

Cascadian Farm -

Organic Frozen

Country Style Potatoes

Crinkle Cut French Fries

Hash Browns

Shoe String Fries

Spud Puppies

Straight Cut French Fries

Wedge Cut Oven Fries

Great Value Brand (Wal-Mart) -

Canned (Diced, Sliced, Whole)

P

Instant Mashed Potatoes

Hy-Vee - Frozen (Country Style Hash Brown Potatoes)

Ian's - Alphatots, Supertots

Meijer Brand - Canned White (Sliced, Whole), Frozen French Fries (Quickie Crinkles)

Ore-Ida -

Frozen

Hash Browns (9 Count, Country Style, Southern Style)

Potatoes O'Brien

Publix - Frozen Hash Browns (Country Style, Southern Style)

Safeway Brand -

Hashbrowns (Country Style, Southern Style)

O'Brien

Spartan Brand -

Mashed Potatoes (Instant)

White (Sliced, Whole Sliced)

Sunny Select - Canned (Whole), Sliced

Tasty Bite - Bombay

Wegmans Brand -

Frozen Hash Browns

Country Style

Hash Browns O'Brien

Regular

Potatoes (Sliced, Whole)

Woodstock Farms -

Organic Frozen

Crinkle Cut Oven Fries

Shredded Hash Browns

Tastee Taters

Preserves... see Jam/Jelly

P

Pretzels

Ener-G -

Crispy Pretzels

Wylde Pretzels (Poppy Seed, Regular, Sesame)

Protein

Nutiva -

Hemp Protein Shake

Amazon Acai

Berry Pomegrate

Chocolate

Protein Powder (Hemp, Plain)

Protein Shakes... see Shakes &... see Protein

Prunes

Great Value Brand (Wal-Mart) - Pitted Prunes

Meijer Brand - Pitted (Canister, Carton)

Spartan Brand - Prunes Pitted

Pudding

Jell-O -

Instant Pudding & Pie Filling

Chocolate

Regular Cook n Serve

Banana Cream

Chocolate (Fudge, Regular)

Coconut Cream

Vanilla

Regular Instant

Banana Cream

Chocolate (Fudge, Regular)

Coconut Cream

Devil's Food (Fat Free)

French Vanilla

Lemon

Pistachio
Vanilla
White Chocolate (Fat Free)
Sugar Free Fat Free Cook n Serve
Chocolate
Vanilla

Pumpkin... **All **Fresh** Pumpkin Is **Gluten/Casein/Soy-Free***

Libby's -
Canned
100% Pure Pumpkin
Easy Pumpkin Pie Mix
Meijer Brand - Canned
Spartan Brand
Wegmans Brand - Solid Pack

Puppodums

Sharwood's - Indian Puppodums

Q

Quinoa

Arrowhead Mills - Quinoa
Woodstock Farms - Organic White Quinoa

R

Radishes... **All **Fresh** Radishes Are **Gluten/Casein/Soy-Free***

Raisins

365 Organic Every Day Value - Organic Thompson Raisins
Great Value Brand (Wal-Mart) -
California Sun Dried Raisins (100% Natural)

R

Hy-Vee - California Sun Dried Raisins
Meijer Brand - Canister, Seedless (Carton)
Spartan Brand - Regular
Sun-Maid - Baking, Golden, Regular
Sunny Select
Whole Kids Organics - Seedless Thompson, Raisins
Woodstock Farms -
Organic Jumbo Flame
Thompson (Jumbo, Select)

Raspberries... **All **Fresh** Raspberries Are **Gluten/Casein/Soy -Free***
Cascadian Farm - Organic Frozen Raspberries
Hy-Vee - Frozen Red Raspberries
Meijer Brand -
Organic
Red Individually Quick Frozen
Regular
Spartan Brand - Red Raspberries
Woodstock Farms - Organic Frozen Red Raspberries

Raspberry Vinaigrette... see Salad Dressing

Red Peppers... **All **Fresh** Red Peppers Are **Gluten/Casein-Free**

Refried Beans... see Beans

Relish
B&G -
Dill
Emerald
Hamburger
Hot Dog
India
Piccalilli
Sweet
Unsalted
Bubbies - Relish

R

Hy-Vee - Dill, Squeeze Sweet, Sweet
Meijer Brand - Sweet & Dill
Midwest Country Fare - Sweet Pickle
Spartan Brand - Dill, Sweet
Vlasic - Homestyle Dill Relish, Sweet Relish
Wegmans Brand - Dill, Hamburger, Hot Dog Pickle, Sweet
Woodstock Farms - Organic Sweet Relish

Ribs... **All **Fresh** Meat Is **Gluten/Casein/Soy -Free** **(Non-Marinated, Unseasoned)***
Homestyle Meals -
Frozen Fully Cooked Baby Back
Pork Baby Back w/BBQ Sauce
Saz's - Award Winning Baby Back Pork Ribs

Rice
A Taste of Thai - Rice (Jasmine)
Annie Chuns -
Sprouted Brown Rice
Sticky White Rice
Arrowhead Mills -
Brown Basmati
Long Grain Brown
Short Brown
White Basmati
Eden -
Organic Canned
Rice & Cajun Small Red Beans
Rice & Caribbean Black Beans
Rice & Garbanzo Beans
Rice & Kidney Beans
Rice & Lentils
Rice & Pinto Beans

Fantastic World Foods -
- Arborio
- Basmati
- Jasmine

Go Go Rice -
- On The Go Cooked Rice Bowls Steamed Organic
  - Brown Rice
  - Rice Medley
  - White Rice

Gluten-Free Essentials -
- Cherry Jubilee
- Country Apple Cinnamon
- Exotic Curry
- Italian Herb & Lemon
- Southwest Chipotle & Lime

Great Value Brand (Wal-Mart) -
- Enriched Long Grain (Parboiled Rice, Rice Extra Fancy)

Hy-Vee -
- Boil In Bag Rice
- Enriched Extra Long Grain (Instant, Regular)
- Extra Long Grain
- Instant Brown
- Natural Long Grain Brown

Kraft Minute Rice - Boil In Bag, Brown, Premium, White

Lundberg -
- Rice Blends
  - Black Japonica
  - Countrywild
  - Jubilee
  - Olde World Pilaf
  - Wehani
  - Wild Blend

RiceXpress (Chicken Herb, Classic Beef)
White Eco Farmed California (Arborio, Basmati, Jasmine)
White Organic California
Arborio
Basmati
Jasmine
Sushi
Whole Grain Brown Eco Farmed
California Basmati
Long Grain
Short Grain
Whole Grain Brown Organic
Brown Sweet
California Basmati
California Jasmine
Golden Rose
Long Grain
Short Grain
Wild Rice Blends
Organic
Quick
Wild
Wild & Wehani
Wild & White Basmati

Meijer Brand -
Brown
Instant (Boil In Bag, Brown, White)
White Long Grain
White Medium Grain

Minute Rice - Brown, White

Nishiki - Sushi Rice

R

Publix -
Long Grain (Enriched, Whole Grain Brown)
Pre Cooked Instant (Boil in Bag, Brown, White)
Safeway Brand - Enriched Calrose, Instant, Long Grain, White
Spartan Brand -
Instant
Boil In Bag
Brown Box
Regular Box
4% Broken Long Grain
Success -
Boil In Bag
Jasmine Rice
Natural Long Grain Brown Rice
White Rice
Whole Grain Brown Rice
Sunny Select - Regular (Brown, White)
Tasty Bite - Sprouts Curry & Basmati Rice
Thai Kitchen - Jasmine Rice
Trader Joe's -
All Grain Rice
Organic (All Grain Rice)
Rice Pilaf
Uncle Ben's -
Boil In Bag
Converted Brand Rice
Fast & Natural Whole Grain
Whole Grain Brown
Wegmans Brand -
Arborio
Basmati

Boil In Bag
Enriched (Long, Long Grain White)
Instant (Brown, Regular)
Jasmine
Long Grain (Brown, Regular)
Medium Grain White

Rice Beverages

Amazake -
Almond
Amazing Mango
Banana Appeal
Cool Coconut
Go (Go Green, Hazelnuts)
Oh So Original
Rice Nog
Tiger Chai
Vanilla Pecan Pie

Good Karma -
Organic Ricemilk
Chocolate
Original
Vanilla

Pacific Foods - Low Fat Rice Beverage (Plain, Vanilla)

Rice Dream -
Enriched (Organic Original, Chocolate, Vanilla)
Refrigerated Enriched Rice Drink (Original, Vanilla)
Shelf Stable Rice Drink
Classic (Carob, Vanilla)
Enriched (Original, Vanilla)
Heartwise (Original, Vanilla)
Horchata

Original
Supreme (Chocolate Chai, Vanilla Hazelnut)
Wegmans Brand - Original, Vanilla
Rice Bread... see Bread
Rice Cakes
Lundberg -
Eco Farmed Classic
Brown Rice (Lightly Salted, Salt Free)
Eco Farmed Savory
Toasted Sesame
Eco Farmed Sweet
Apple Cinnamon
Organic Classic
Brown Rice (Lightly Salted, Salt Free)
Mochi Sweet
Rice w/Popcorn
Wild Rice
Rice Cream
Erewhon - Brown Rice Cream
Rice Noodles... see Noodles
Rice Shakes... see Rice Beverages or Shakes
Rice Syrup
Lundberg Organic -
Eco Farmed Sweet Dreams
Organic Sweet Dreams
Rice Thins
Eden - Brown Rice Chips
Sesmark - Brown Rice
Rice Vinegar... see Vinegar
Risotto
Lundberg - Organic (Florentine, Tuscan)
Roast Beef... see Beef

Rolls... **see Bread**
Rum... **All **Distilled** Alcohol Is **Gluten/Casein/Soy-Free*** [2]
Rusks
 Glutino - Gluten Free Rusks
Rutabaga... **All **Fresh** Rutabaga Is **Gluten/Casein/Soy-Free***

S

Salad... **All **Fresh** Salad Is **Gluten/Casein/Soy-Free***
 Trader Joe's - Baby Spinach Salad
Salad Dressing
 Annie's Naturals -
  Natural Dressings
   Lemon & Chive
   Light Italian
   Low Fat Vinaigrette (Honey Mustard, Raspberry)
   Mango Fat Free
   Roasted Red Pepper Vinaigrette
   Strawberry & Balsamic Fat Free
   Tuscany Italian
  Organic
   Green Garlic
   Maple Ginger
   Oil & Vinegar
   Raspberry & Balsamic Fat-Free
   Roasted Garlic
 Bragg - Organic (Ginger & Sesame, Vinaigrette)
 Briannas -
  Dijon Honey Mustard
  New American

[2] www.celiac.com

Rich (Poppy Seed, Santa Fe Blend)
Vinaigrette (Blush Wine)
Consorzio -
Fat Free
Mango
Raspberry & Balsamic
Strawberry & Balsamic
Drew's All Natural -
Garlic Italian
Honey Dijon
Kalamata Olive & Caper
Poppy Seed
Raspberry
Roasted Garlic & Peppercorn
Rosemary Balsamic
Smoked Tomato
Emeril's - Dressing (Caesar, House Herb Vinaigrette)
Fischer & Wieser -
Original Roasted Raspberry Chipotle Vinaigrette
Follow Your Heart -
Caesar
Girard's -
Fat Free
Balsamic Vinaigrette
Raspberry
Red Wine Vinaigrette
Ken's Steak House -
Fat Free Dressings (Raspberry Pecan, Sun Dried Tomato)
Lite Dressings (Raspberry Walnut)
Kraft -
Free French
Light Balsamic Vinaigrette

Zesty Italian

Lettuce in Love -

Caesar

Skinny Italian

Sweet Balsamic

Thousand Island

Maple Grove Farms of Vermont -

All Natural

Blueberry Pomegranate

Champagne Vinaigrette

Ginger Pear

Maple Fig

Strawberry Balsamic

Fat Free

Cranberry Balsamic

Greek

Honey Dijon

Lime Basil

Vinaigrette (Balsamic, Raspberry)

Organic

Dijon

Italian Herb

Vinaigrette (Balsamic, Raspberry)

Regular & Lite

Balsamic Maple

Sweet N' Sour

Sugar Free

Italian Balsamic

Vinaigrette (Balsamic, Raspberry)

Marzetti -

Pourable Dressings

Italian (Fat Free)
Sweet 'N Sour (Fat Free)

Newman's Own -
Light
Balsamic Vinaigrette
Italian
Raspberry & Walnut
Red Wine Vinegar & Olive Oil
Roasted Garlic Balsamic
Organic Light Balsamic Vinaigrette
Regular
Olive Oil & Vinegar
Parisienne Dijon Lime
Two Thousand Island

Pfeiffer -
Pourable Dressings
Fat Free Italian

Teresa's -
Select Recipes Salad Dressings
Fat Free Honey Dijon

Trader Joe's - Tuscan Italian w/Balsamic Vinegar

Walden Farms -
Sugar Free No Carb
Balsamic Vinaigrette
Coleslaw
Creamy (Bacon, Garlic Ranch, Italian)
French
Honey Dijon
Italian w/Sun Dried Tomato
Jersey Sweet Onion
Raspberry Vinaigrette
Russian

Thousand Island
Zesty Italian
Wegmans Brand -
Fat Free (Red Wine Vinegar, Roasted Red Pepper)

Salami... see Sausage and/or Deli Meat

Salmon... see Fish **All **Fresh** Salmon Is **Gluten/Casein/Soy-Free** **(Non-Marinated, Unseasoned)***

Crown Prince - Pink (Fancy Alaskan)
Crown Prince Natural -
Alaskan Pink
Alder Wood Smoked Alaskan Coho
Skinless & Boneless Pacific Pink
Great Value Brand (Wal-Mart) -
Canned (Alaskan Pink Salmon)
Kroger Brand - Canned
Whole Catch -
Cold Smoked (Regular, Wild Sockeye)
Sockeye Fillet
Wild Sockeye

Salsa

Amy's -
Organic
Black Bean & Corn
Fire Roasted Vegetable
Mild
Spicy Chipotle
Bone Suckin' Salsa - Hot, Regular
Chi-Chi's - Fiesta, Original
Dei Fratelli - Original
Drew's -
Organic
Chipotle Lime (Medium)

Double Roasted (Medium)
Regular (Hot, Medium, Mild)
Eat Smart - Garden Style Sweet
Fischer & Wieser -
Das Peach Haus Peach
Salsa A La Charra
Salsa Verde Ranchera
Frontera -
Chipotle
Habanero
Roasted
Guajillo
Jalapeno Cilantro
Poblano
Red Pepper & Garlic/Tomato
Tomato Cilantro & Mild Red Chiles
Tangy Two Chile
Green Mountain Gringo - All Varieties (Hot Medium, Mild)
Herr's - Chunky (Medium, Mild)
Hy-Vee - Thick & Chunky (Hot, Medium, Mild)
Kroger Brand -
Picante Sauce (Hot, Medium, Mild)
Thick & Chunky (Hot, Medium, Mild)
Traditional (Hot, Medium, Mild)
La Victoria -
Cilantro (Medium, Mild)
Green Salsa Jalapena Extra Hot
Ranchera
Red Jalapeno Extra Hot
Suprema (Medium, Mild)
Thick 'N Chunky
Hot

Medium
Mild
Verde (Medium, Mild)
Victoria
Meijer Brand -
Original (Hot, Medium, Mild)
Restaurant Style (Hot, Medium, Mild)
Santa Fe Style (Medium, Mild)
Thick & Chunky (Hot, Medium, Mild)
Muir Glen -
Medium
Black Bean & Corn
Garlic Cilantro
Regular
Mild
Newman's Own -
Black Bean & Corn
Hot
Mango
Medium
Mild
Organic (Cilantro, Medium)
Peach
Pineapple
Roasted Garlic
Tequila Lime
Old El Paso -
Salsa Thick N' Chunky
Hot
Medium
Mild

Ortega -
- Original
  - Medium
  - Mild
  - Thick & Chunky (Medium, Mild)

Pace -
- Chunky Salsa
  - Chipotle
  - Cilantro
  - Hot
  - Lime & Garlic
  - Medium
  - Mild
- Specialty Salsa
  - Pico De Gallo
  - Salsa Verde
  - Tequila Lime
  - Triple Pepper

Publix -
- All Natural (Hot, Medium, Mild)
- Southwestern Black Bean & Corn
- Thick & Chunky (Hot, Medium, Mild)

Safeway Select -
- Fiesta Fajita
- Garlic Lovers
- Peach Pineapple
- Roasted Tomato
- Salsa Verde
- Southwest

Salpica -
- Cilantro Green Olive
- Fall Harvest

Garlic Chipotle
Habanero Lime
Mango Peach
Roasted Corn & Bean
Rustic Tomato
Spring Break
Summer Of Love

Santa Barbara -
Black Bean & Corn
Chile Relleno
Fire Roasted Chili
Mango & Peach
Peach & Chipotle
Roasted
Garlic
Red Pepper Corn & Black Bean
Tomatillo

Sunny Select - Medium, Mild

Taco Bell - Thick 'n Chunky (Medium, Mild)

Tostitos -
All Natural
Medium (Black Bean & Corn, Picante, Pineapple & Peach, Regular)
Mild (Picante)

Trader Joe's -
Chunky
Corn & Chili
Hot & Smokey Chipotle
Pineapple
Spicy/Smokey Peach
Verde

UTZ - Mt. Misery Mike's Salsa, Sweet Salsa Dip

S

Wegmans Brand -
Hot
Medium
Mild
Organic (Hot, Mango, Medium, Mild)
Roasted (Chipotle, Salsa Verde, Sweet Pepper, Tomato)
Santa Fe Style

Salt

Great Value Brand (Wal-Mart) - Iodized, Plain
Kroger Brand
Marsh Brand - Regular
Meijer Brand - Iodized, Plain
Morton - Coarse Kosher, Iodized, Plain, Sea Salt
Spartan Brand - Garlic, Iodized, Plain
Sunny Select - Iodized
Wegmans Brand - Iodized, Plain

Sandwich Meat... see Deli Meat

Sardines... **All **Fresh** Sardines Are **Gluten/Casein/Soy -Free (Non-Marinated, Unseasoned)***

Bumble Bee - In (Water)
Chicken Of The Sea - In (Tomato Sauce, Water)
Crown Prince -
Crosspacked Brisling In Olive Oil
One Layer Brisling In (Mustard, Spring Water)
Oval Tomato (Hot, Regular)
Regular In (Spring Water, Tomato Sauce)
Skinless & Boneless In (Olive Oil, Water)
Two Layer Brisling In Olive Oil
Crown Prince Natural -
One Layer Brisling In (Mustard, Spring Water)
Skinless & Boneless In Oil (Pure Olive Oil, Water)
Two Layer Brisling In Olive Oil

Ocean Prince -
In (Spring Water, Tomato Sauce)
Reese - In Olive Oil

Sauces... (includes Pasta, Marinara, Tomato, Misc.)

A Taste of Thai -
Garlic Chili Pepper
Peanut (Satay Sauce)
Sweet Red Chili
Amy's -
Family Marinara
Low Sodium Marinara
Roasted Garlic
Tomato Basil
Baxters - Mint Sauce
Bertolli -
Marinara w/Burgundy Wine
Organic Olive Oil & Basil & Garlic
Tomato & Basil
Vidalia Onion w/Roasted Garlic
Bove's Of Vermont -
All Natural (Marinara, Mushroom & Wine, Roasted Garlic)
Organic (Marinara, Roasted Garlic)
Capa Di Roma -
Arrustica
Fresh Basil
Marinara
Roasted Garlic
Classico -
Bruschetta Sauce (Basil & Tomato, Extra Garlic)
Organic (Spinach & Garlic, Tomato/Herbs & Spices)
Roasted Garlic

Spicy (Red Pepper, Tomato & Basil)
Sun Dried Tomato
Tomato & Basil
Traditional Sweet Basil

Contadina -
Deluxe (Marinara, Spaghetti)
Fully Prepared Pizza Sauce
Marinara
Spaghetti

Dave's Gourmet -
Organic
Red Heirloom
Roasted Garlic & Sweet Basil

Di Lusso - Sweet Onion Sauce

Eden -
Spaghetti Sauce
Organic
Organic No Salt Added

Emeril's -
Pasta Sauce
Kicked Up (Green Pepper, Red Pepper, Tomato)
Mushroom & Onion
Puttanesca
Roasted (Red Pepper)
Sicilian Gravy

Follow Your Heart -
Balsamic Barbecue Sauce
Mild
Spicy
Balsamic Vinaigrette Sauce
Original
Unforgettables Low Fat

S

Frank's RedHot -
- Buffalo Wing
- Chile 'n Lime
- Original
- Xtra Hot

Frontera -
- Cocktail & Ceviche Sauce
  - Cilantro Lime
  - Tomato Chipotle
- Cooking Sauce
  - Red Chile & Roasted Garlic
  - Roasted Garlic & Chipotle
  - Tomato & Cilantro
- Enchilada Sauce
  - Chipotle Garlic
  - Classic Red Chile
- Grilling Sauce
  - Chipotle Honey Mustard
  - Red Pepper Sesame
- Hot Sauce
  - Chipotle
  - Habanero
  - Jalapeno
  - Red Pepper
- Taco Sauce
  - Chipotle Garlic
  - Roasted Tomato

Great Value Brand (Wal-Mart) -
- Tomato Sauce

Las Palmas - Red Chili, Red Enchilada

Lee Kum Kee -
Choy Sun Oyster Flavored
Shrimp
Meijer Brand -
Extra Chunky Spaghetti Sauce
Garden Combo
Mushroom & Green Pepper
Pasta Sauce Select
Marinara
Mushroom & Olive
Onion & Garlic
Mr. Spice Organic -
Sauce & Marinade
Ginger Stir Fry
Honey BBQ
Indian Curry
Sweet & Sour
Thai Peanut
Muir Glen -
Organic Pasta Sauce
Cabernet Marinara
Chunky Tomato & Herb
Fire Roasted Tomato
Garden Vegetable
Garlic Roasted Garlic
Italian Herb
Portabello Mushroom
Tomato Basil
Pizza Sauce
Tomato Sauce (Chunky, No Salt Added, Regular)
Newman's Own -
Cabernet Marinara

S

Diavolo (Spicy Simmer Sauce)
Italian Sausage & Peppers
Marinara w/Mushroom
Organic (Marinara, Tomato Basil, Traditional Herb)
Pesto & Tomato
Sweet Onion
Tomato (Basil, w/Roasted Garlic)

Pacific Natural Foods - Tomato Sauce

Palmieri - Fra Diavolo

Prego -
Mushroom ***(4 lb 3 oz. Jar only)***
Organic (All Flavors, All Sizes)
Traditional (All Sizes)

Publix - Tomato Sauce

Ragu - Light (Tomato & Basil)

Safeway Select - Pasta Sauce (Mushroom/Onion)

Sauces 'N Love - Barely Bolognese

Saz's - Vidalia Onion Cooking Sauce

Scarpetta -
Arrabbiata
Barely Bolognese
Bruschetta Topping
Tomato & Caper
Tomato & Artichoke
Marinara
Puttanesca

Seeds Of Change -
Indian Simmer Sauce (Jalfrezi, Madras)
Pasta Sauce
Arrabiatta di Roma
Garden Vegetable Piemonte

Marinara di Venezia
Modena Balsamic & Onion
Porcini Mushroom di Apennine
Puttanesca Napoletana
Sicilian Spicy Eggplant
Tomato Basil Genovese
Tuscan Tomato & Garlic

Spartan Brand - Sloppy Joe, Tomato Sauce

Stonewall Kitchen Sauce -
Roasted Garlic Basil
Traditional Marinara

Sunny Select - Hearty Vegetable, Marinara

Thai Kitchen -
Fish Sauce
Simmer Sauce (Green, Panang, Red)
Spicy Thai Chili Sauce
Sweet Red Chili Sauce

Trader Joe's -
Pasta Sauce
Curry Simmer
Mango
Pizza Fat Free
Rustico
Tuscano Marinara Sauce Low Fat

Walnut Acres -
Garlic Garlic
Low Sodium Tomato Basil
Marinara & Zinfandel
Marinara w/Herbs
Roasted Garlic
Sweet Pepper & Onion
Tomato & Basil

Tomato & Mushroom
Zesty Basil
Wegmans Brand -
Bruschetta Topping (Traditional Tomato)
Prepared Horseradish
Tomato (Regular)
Wild Thymes - Tropical Mango Lime Sauce
Sauerkraut
Bubbies
Eden - Organic
Hy-Vee - Shredded Kraut
Krrrrisp Kraut - Bavarian, Regular
S&W - All Varieties
Silver Floss - Bavarian, Regular
Spartan Brand
Wegmans Brand
Sausage -
Aidells -
Artichoke & Garlic
Bier
Cajun Style Andouille (Minis, Regular)
Chicken & Apple (Minis, Regular)
Habanero & Green Chile
Mango (Regular)
Maple & Smoked Bacon Breakfast Links
Roasted Red Pepper w/Corn
Smoked Chorizo
Sun Dried Tomato (Minis, Regular)
Whiskey Fennel
Applegate Farms -
Breakfast Sausage
Chicken & Apple Sunday

Chicken & Sage Sunday
Coppa
Genoa Salami (Hot, Organic, Regular)
Hot Dogs (Beef, Big Apple, Chicken, Turkey)
Joy Stick
Organic
Andouille
Chicken & Apple
Fire Roasted Red Pepper
Sweet Italian
Pork (Andouille, Bratwurst, Kielbasa)
Organic Hot Dogs
Beef
Chicken
Cocktail Franks
Great Organic
Stadium Style
Turkey
Pancetta
Sopressata (Hot, Regular)
Uncured (Pepperoni, Prosciutto)
Di Lusso - Prosciutto Ham
Dietz & Watson -
Sausage & Lunchmeat
Bratwurst
Honey Roll
Knockwurst
Lunch Roll
New York Style Deli Beef Franks
Pepper & Onion Sausage
Prosciutto Classico
Wieners

Ejays So. Smokehouse -
Smoke Jalapeno
Smoked Kielbasa
Global Gourmet -
Chicken Sausage
Andouille
Apple Oven Roasted
Chipotle Pepper
Spicy Italian Style
Sun Dried Tomato & Fresh Basil
Great Value Brand (Wal-Mart) - Canned Vienna Sausage
Hillshire Farms -
Lit'l Beef Franks
Lit'l Polskas
Lit'l Smokies
Beef
Chipotle Hot w/Chipotle Peppers
Lite w/Pork/Turkey/Beef
Original
Lit'l Wieners
Smoked Sausage (Turkey)
Honeysuckle White -
Turkey Sausage Rolls (Breakfast, Mild Italian)
Turkey Sausages
Bratwurst
Breakfast Sausage (Links, Patties)
Italian Sausage (Hot, Sweet)
Hy-Vee - Bratwurst Grill Pack
Jimmy Dean -
Bold Country Pork Sausage (Bold, Hot)
Pork Sausage (50% Less Fat, Hot, Italian, Regular, Sage)
Premium Pork Country Sausage (Extra Mild, Mild)

S

Sausage
Fully Cooked Links (Original, Turkey)
Fully Cooked Patties
Hot
Original
Sandwich Size
Turkey
Links (Original)
Patties (Original)

Johnsonville -

Bratwurst
Heat & Serve
Hot 'n Spicy
Original
Smoked
Stadium Style
Chorizo
Hearty Beef Bologna
Home Style Breakfast Patties
Irish O'Garlic
Italian (Heat & Serve, Hot, Mild, Sweet)
Italian Ground Sausage (Hot, Mild, Sweet)
New Orleans Brand Smoked
Original (Breakfast (Links, Patties), Ring Bologna)
Polish
Summer Sausage
Beef
Garlic
Old World Summer
Original
Vermont Maple Syrup (Links, Patties)

Nature's Promise -
Italian Spicy Pork
Mild Italian Chicken
Spiced Apple Chicken
Sun Dried Tomato & Basil Chicken
Oscar Mayer - Beef Franks (Bun Length, Regular)
Primo Naturale -
Chorizo
Dried Hot
Sliced Dried
Sliced Hot
Stick Dried
Chub Salami
Hard
w/Black Pepper
w/Herbs
w/Wine
Pepperoni (Dried, Sliced Dried)
Sliced Salami
Coppa
Hard
Original w/Wine
Premium Genoa
w/Black Pepper
w/Herbs
Sopressata (Regular, Sliced)
Sweet Abruzzi Sausage
Publix -
Fresh Turkey Italian (Mild)
Jumbo Beef Franks

Jumbo Franks
Sausages Italian (Hot, Mild)

Shelton's -
Beef Sticks
Bologna (Uncured Chicken, Uncured Turkey)
Franks
Smoked Chicken
Smoked Turkey
Uncured Chicken
Uncured Turkey
Turkey Sausage (Breakfast, Italian, Patties)
Turkey Sticks (Pepperoni, Regular)

Wegmans Brand -
Beef Hot Dogs (Skinless)
Uncured Beef Hot Dogs (Skinless)

Wellshire Farms -
Beef Franks Hot Dogs (The Old Fashioned, The Premium)
Bratwurst (Original, Smoked, Spicy Hot Style)
Chicken Hot Dogs
Frozen
Beef Hamburgers
Chicken Apple Sausage (Links, Patties)
Country Sage Sausage (Links, Patties)
Original Breakfast Sausage (Links, Patties)
Sunrise Maple Sausage (Links, Patties)
Morning Maple Turkey Breakfast Link Sausage
NY Style Big Beef Franks
Old Fashioned Deli Style Beef Salami
Original Matt's Select Pepperoni Steaks
Polska Kielbasa
Pork Andouille Sausage
Pork Sausage

Chorizo
Linguica
w/Green Peppers & Onions
Sliced (Beef Pepperoni, Cooked Salami)
Smoked Pork Kielbasa Links
The Original Deli Franks
Turkey
Tom Toms (Hot & Spicy, Original)
Wranglers - Franks

Scallops... **All **Fresh** Scallops Are **Gluten/Casein/Soy-Free (Non-Marinated, Unseasoned)***

Seafood Sauce

Frontera -
Cocktail & Ceviche Sauce
Cilantro Lime
Tomato Chipotle
McCormick - Cajun, Mediterranean, Santa Fe Style
Trader Joe's - Seafood Cocktail Sauce

Seasoning Packets... see Seasonings

Seasonings

365 Every Day Value - Berber Ground Coriander, Brazilian Arrowroot, Catalina Cream of Tartar, Cayenne Pepper, Crushed Red Chili Peppers, Ground Nutmeg, Herbes de Provence, Jamaican Allspice, Sea Salt, Sea Salt Fine Crystals, Spanish Rosemary, Spanish Wild Thyme, Sweet Paprika, Turkish Bay Leaves, Valle del Sol Chile Powder, Whole Sesame Seeds

365 Organic Every Day Value - Basil, Black Pepper, Black Peppercorns, Cinnamon, Cumin, Garlic Powder, Ginger, Minced Onion, Oregano, Parsley, Turmeric

Accent - Flavor Enhancer

S

Arora Creations -
Organic Seasoning Packets (Bhindi Masala, Gobi, Punjabi Chhole, Rajmah, Tandoori Chicken)
Regular Seasoning Packets (Bhindi Masala, Goan Fish, Gobi, Punjabi Chhole, Rajmah, Tandoori Chicken, Tikka Masala)

Bragg - Sprinkle Seasoning

Durkee - Allspice, Alum, Anise Seed, Arrowroot, Basil, Bay Leaves, Caraway Seeds, Cardamom, Cayenne Pepper, Celery Seed, Chicken Seasoning, Chili Powder, Chives, Cilantro, Cinnamon, Citrus Grill, Cloves, Coriander, Cream of Tartar, Crushed Red Pepper, Cumin, Curry Powder, Dill Seed/Weed, Fennel, Garlic Minced, Garlic Powder, Garlic Salt, Ginger, Italian Seasoning, Jamaican Jerk Seasoning, Lemon Pepper, Lime Pepper, MSG, Mace, Marjoram, Meat Tenderizer, Mint Leaves, Mustard, Nutmeg, Onion Minced, Onion Powder, Onion Salt, Oregano, Paprika, Parsley, Pepper (All), Pepper Green Bell, Pickling Spice, Poppyseed, Poultry Seasoning, Pumpkin Pie Spice, Rosemary, Sage, Sesame Seed, Tarragon, Thyme, Turmeric

Emeril's -
Essence (Asian, Bayou Blast, Italian, Original, Southwest)
Steak Rub

Hy-Vee - Basil Leaf, Bay Leaves, Black Pepper, Chicken Grill Seasoning, Chili Powder, Chopped Onion, Dill Weed, Garlic Powder, Garlic Salt, Ground Cinnamon, Ground Cloves, Ground Mustard, Iodized Salt, Italian Seasoning, Lemon Pepper, Meat Tenderizer, Oregano Leaf, Paprika, Parsley Flakes, Plain Salt, Red Crushed Pepper, Rosemary, Salt & Pepper Shaker, Seasoned Salt, Steak Grilling Seasoning, Thyme

Lawry's -
- Packets (Guacamole, Mexican Rice, Tenderizing Beef Marinade Mix)
- Seasoning (Black Pepper Seasoned Salt, Garlic Pepper, Lemon Pepper, Salt Free 17, Seasoned Pepper)

McCormick -
- Grill Mates Seasoning (Montreal Chicken, Montreal Steak)
- Spices (Alum, Anise Seed, Apple Pie Spice, Basil Leaves, Bay Leaves, Caraway Seed, Celery Flakes, Celery Seed, Chili Powder, Chives, Cilantro Leaves, Cinnamon Sticks, Cinnamon Sugar, Cream of Tartar, Cumin Seed, Curry Powder, Dill Seed, Dill Weed, Fennel Seed, Ground Allspice, Ground Cinnamon, Ground Cloves, Ground Cumin, Ground Ginger, Ground Mace, Ground Marjoram, Ground Mustard, Ground Nutmeg, Ground Oregano, Ground Sage, Ground Thyme, Ground Turmeric, Hot Mexican Style, Italian Seasoning, Marjoram Leaves, Mixed Pickling Spice, Mustard Seed, Oregano (Oregano Entero), Oregano Leaves, Paprika, Parsley Flakes, Poppy Seed, Poultry Seasoning, Pumpkin Pie Spice, Rosemary Leaves, Rubbed Sage, Sage Leaves, Sesame Seed, Tarragon Leaves, Whole Allspice, Whole Cloves, Whole Mexican)

Meijer Brand -
- Black Pepper, Chili Powder, Cinnamon, Garlic Powder, Garlic Salt, Minced Onion, Onion Salt, Oregano Leaves, Paprika, Parsley Flakes

Mortons
- Light Salt Mixture
- Nature's Seasoning Blend
- Sausage & Meat Loaf Seasoning
- Sugar Cure (Plain)

Tender Quick

Mrs. Dash - Original

Nantucket Off-Shore - Rub (Bayou, Dragon, Holiday Turkey, Mt. Olympus, Nantucket, Prairie, Pueblo, Rasta, Renaissance, St. Remy), Summer Shellfish Boil

Nielsen-Massy - Madagascar Bourbon Pure Vanilla Powder

O Organics - Basil, Bay Leaves, Rosemary, Sage, Thyme

Old Bay - Seasoning

Publix Brand - Adobo Seasoning with Pepper, Adobo Seasoning without Pepper, Black Pepper, Chili Powder, Garlic Powder, Garlic Salt, Ground Ginger, Ground Red Pepper, Lemon & Pepper, Minced Onion, Parsley Flakes, Seasoned Salt, Whole Basil Leaves, Whole Bay Leaves, Whole Black Pepper, Whole Oregano

Safeway Brand - Fajita Seasoning Mix

Shaw's Brand - Basil Leaves, Black Pepper, Celery Salt, Chili Powder, Cinnamon, Garlic Powder, Garlic Salt, Minced Onion, Onion Powder, Oregano Leaves, Paprika, Parsley Flakes

Spartan Brand - Black Pepper, Chili Powder, Cinnamon, Garlic Powder, Garlic Salt, Ground Nutmeg, Iodized Salt, Minced Onion, Oregano Leaves, Paprika, Parsley Flakes, Salt, Vanilla Extract

Spice Islands - Allspice (Ground, Whole), Ancho Chile, Anise Seed, Arrowroot, Basil, Bay Leaves, Beau Monde Seasoning, Caraway Seed, Cardamom, Cayenne Pepper, Celery Salt, Celery Seed, Chili Powder, Chipotle Chile Seasoning, Chives, Cilantro, Cinnamon, Cloves, Coriander, Cream of Tartar, Cumin, Curry Powder, Dill Weed, Fennel, Garam Masala, Garlic & Herb, Garlic Pepper, Garlic Powder, Garlic Salt, Ginger, Greek, Ground Chipotle Chile, Ground

Ginger, Herbes De Provence, Italian Herb Seasoning, Jamaican Jerk Seasoning, Leaf Oregano, Lemon Peel, Lemon Pepper, Louisiana Style Cajun Seasoning, Marjoram, Mediterranean, Mint, Mustard, Nutmeg, Onion Minced, Onion Powder, Onion Salt, Orange Peel, Oregano, Paprika, Pepper, Pepper Black, Pesto, Poppyseed, Poultry Seasoning, Pumpkin Pie Spice, Red Pepper, Rosemary, Rosemary Garlic, Saffron, Sage, Sesame Seeds, Smoked Paprika, Spicy Chicken Seasoning, Summer Savory, Sweet Basil, Tarragon, Thai Seasoning, Thyme, Turmeric, Vanilla Bean

Spice Islands Specialty - Beau Monde, Garlic Pepper Seasoning, Italian Herb Seasoning, Saffron, Vanilla Bean

Tones - Allspice, Alum, Anise Seed, Arrowroot, Basil, Bay Leaves, Caraway Seeds, Cardamom, Cayenne Pepper, Celery Flakes, Celery Seed, Chicken Seasoning, Chili Powder, Chives, Cilantro, Cinnamon, Cloves, Coriander, Cream of Tartar, Crushed Red Pepper, Cumin, Curry Powder, Dill Seed/Weed, Fennel, Garlic Minced, Garlic Powder, Garlic Salt, Ginger, Ground Black Pepper, Ground Cinnamon, Ground Cumin, Hickory Smoke Salt, Italian Seasoning, Jamaican Jerk Seasoning, Lemon & Herb, Lemon Garlic Seasoning, Lime Pepper, MSG, Mace, Marjoram, Minced Onion, Mint Leaves, Mustard, Nutmeg, Onion Minced, Onion Powder, Onion Salt, Orange Peel, Oregano, Paprika, Parsley, Pepper (All), Pepper Green Bell, Pickling Spice, Poppyseed, Poultry Seasoning, Pumpkin Pie Spice, Rosemary, Rosemary Garlic, Sage, Seasoned Pepper, Sesame Seed, Spicy Spaghetti, Tarragon, Thyme, Turmeric, Whole Black Peppercorns

Trader Joe's - All Spices

S

Tropical Sun Spices - Caribbean Garlic Lemon Herb, Caribbean Guava Delite, Caribbean Seasoning Salt, Caribbean Tangerine Pepper, Citrus Delite Spice, Creole Spice, Cuban Rum Spice, Salsa Seasoning Spice, Southwest Santa Fe Spice, Strawberry Spice Rub, Sun Fisherman's Seasoning

Weber Grill Creations - Black Peppercorn Marinade Mix, Chicago Steak Seasoning, Cracked Black Pepper & Herb, Sweet 'N Savory Salmon, Smokey Mesquite

Wegmans Brand - Cracked Pepper Blend, Fleur De Sel (Sea Salt), Herbes De Provence, Lemon Pepper Seasoning, Pepper Black

Seaweed

Nagai's - Sushi Nori Roasted Seaweed

Yaki - Sushi Nori Roasted Seaweed

Seeds

365 Every Day Value - Raw Sunflower

Frito Lay - Flamin' Hot Flavored Sunflower Seeds, Sunflower Seeds

Publix - Sunflower Seeds

Spartan Brand - Sunflower Kernels

Trader Joe's - Pumpkin & Pepitas, Sunflower

Woodstock Farms -

Organic Seeds

Flax

Pumpkin (Regular, Roasted Salted)

Sesame

Sunflower (Regular, Roasted Salted)

Sesame Oil... see Oil

Sesame Seeds... see Seeds

Shakes

Amazake -

Almond

Amazing Mango

Banana Appeal

Go Hazelnuts

Oh So Original

Rice Nog

Tiger Chai

Vanilla Pecan Pie

Shortening

Spectrum - Organic Palm Oil Shortening

Shrimp... **All **Fresh** Shrimp Is **Gluten/Casein/Soy-Free (Non-Marinated, Unseasoned)***

Bumble Bee -

Regular (Broken, Jumbo, Large, Medium, Small)

Tiny

Deveined

Large

Medium

Small

Crown Prince - Shrimp (Broken, Tiny)

Great Value Brand (Wal-Mart) - Canned Tiny Shrimp

Trader Joe's - Shrimp Stir Fry

Whole Catch -

Cooked

Raw

Wild Key West Pink (Shell On, Tail Off)

Shrimp Sauce... **see Cocktail Sauce**

Sloppy Joe/Sloppy Joe Sauce

Hormel - Not So Sloppy Joe

Hy-Vee - Sloppy Joe

S

Meijer Brand - Sloppy Joe Sauce
Spartan Brand - Sloppy Joe Sauce

Smoke

Colgin -
All Natural Liquid Smoke
Apple
Hickory
Mesquite
Pecan

Smoked Sausage... see Sausage
Smoked Turkey... see Turkey

Snacks

Amaranth (Nu-World Foods) -
Mini Ridges (Rosemary Basil, Sun Dried Tomato)
Snackers (BBQ Sweet Sassy, Chili Lime, French Onion)
Baken-Ets - Fried Pork Skins
Baffles - Snack Clusters (BBQ)
Betty Lou's - Krispy Bites
Eden - All Mixed Up (Regular), Wild Berry Mix
Fritos - Corn Chips (Original, Scoops)
Herr's -
Pork Rinds (BBQ Flavored, Original)
Potato Sticks
Hy-Vee -
Strawberry Fruit Rolls
Tropical Trail Mix
Kellogg's - Fruit Flavored Snacks
Lay's -
Potato Chips
Classic
Deli Style Original

Kettle Cooked (Reduced Fat Original)
Light Original
Lightly Salted
Maui Style (Regular)
Natural
Country BBQ Thick Cut
Sea Salt Thick Cut
Wavy Potato Chips
Regular
Maui Style - Potato Chips (Regular)
Meijer Brand -
Fruit Rolls
Justice League Berry
Rescue Heroes
Strawberry (Garfield, Regular)
Wildberry Rush
Fruit Snacks
Curious George
Justice League (Big Box, Regular)
Mixed Fruit
Peanuts
Rescue Heroes Big Box
Variety Pack (Big Boy, Regular)
Veggie Tales
Miss Vickie's -
Kettle Cooked Potato Chips
Simply Sea Salt
Smokehouse BBQ
Mrs. May's Naturals -
Crunch
Almond

Black Sesame
Cashew
Coconut Almond
Cran Blueberry
Cran Tropical
Pecan
Pumpkin
Strawberry Pineapple
Sunflower
Walnut
White Sesame
Fruit Chips (Regular, Sugarless)
Apple
Peach
Pear
Pineapple
Nu-World Foods (Amaranth) -
Mini Ridges
Cheddar
Rosemary Basil
Sun Dried Tomato
Snackers
BBQ Sweet Sassy
Chili Lime
French Onion
Robert's American Gourmet -
Baked Tings
Booty (Simply)
Potato Flyers (Original)
Tings

Ruffles -
Potato Chips
Natural (Reduced Fat, Regular, Sea Salted)
Original (Light, Reduced Fat, Regular)
Schar -
Crackers
Crisp Rolls
Fette Biscottate
Fette Croccanti
Grissini
Salti
Tostitos -
Tortilla Chips
Light Restaurant Style
Natural Corn Restaurant Style (Blue, Yelow)
True North -
Clusters
Almond
Peanut
Pecan Almond Peanut
Wise -
Onion Flavored Rings
Pork Rinds (Hot & Spice BBQ, Original)
Woodstock Farms -
Cranberry (Walnut Cashew)
Goji Berry Power
Organic (Snack Mix Campfire)
Tropical (Delight)

Snaps

Edward and Sons -
Brown Rice Snaps
Onion Garlic

Salsa
Toasted Onion
Unsalted Plain
Unsalted Sesame
Vegetable

Soda Pop/Carbonated Beverages

7up - All Varieties
A & W - Root Beer
Aquafina -
FlavorSplash (Citrus Blend, Raspberry, Wild Berry)
Sparkling (Berry Burst, Citrus Twist)
Canada Dry -
Club Soda (All Varieties)
Ginger Ale (Diet, Green Tea Ginger Ale, Regular)
Tonic Water (All Varieties)
Coca-Cola -
Blak
Cherry Coke
Diet
Regular
Zero
Classic Coke
Caffeine Free
Regular
w/Lime, Zero
Diet Coke
Caffeine Free
Plus
Regular
Sweetened w/Lime
w/Splenda
Vanilla Coke

Regular
Zero
Dr. Pepper -
Caffeine Free (Diet, Regular)
Cherry Vanilla (Diet, Regular)
Diet
Regular
Hires - Root Beer
Hy-Vee Soda -
Cherry Cola
Cola (Diet, Regular)
Cream Soda
Dr. Hy-Vee
Fruit Punch (Regular)
Grape
Hee Haw (Diet, Regular)
Lemon Lime
Root Beer (Diet)
Strawberry
Water Cooler
Black Cherry
Key Lime
Kiwi Strawberry
Mixed Berry
Peach
Peach Melba
Raspberry
Strawberry
White Grape
I.B.C. - Root Beer
Meijer Brand -
Encore (Blue (Diet, Regular)

- Cherry (Diet, Regular)
- Red (Diet, Regular)
- Red

Orangina - Sparkling Citrus Beverage

Pepsi -

- Caffeine Free Pepsi (Diet, Regular)
- Diet Pepsi Jazz
- Lime (Diet, Regular)
- One
- Pepsi (Diet, Regular)
- Sierra Mist (Free, Regular)

Publix -

- Black Cherry Soda
- Cherry Cola
- Club Soda
- Cola (Caffeine Free, Regular)
- Cream soda
- Diet
    - Black Cherry Soda
    - Cola
    - Ginger Ale
    - Root Beer
    - Tonic Water
- Dr. Publix
- Ginger Ale
- Grape Soda
- Lemon Lime (Seltzer, Soda)
- Raspberry Seltzer
- Root Beer
- Seltzer Water
- Strawberry

Tonic Water

Schweppes -

Club Soda

Dry Grape Ginger Ale

Ginger Ale (Diet, Regular)

Tonic Water (Diet, Regular)

Sierra Mist

Cranberry Splash (Free, Regular)

Free

Regular

Slice -

Diet Orange

Grape

Orange

Peach

Strawberry

Sprite - Diet, Regular, Zero

Trader Joe's Fresh -

Organic (Sparkling Grapefruit, Sparkling Lemon)

Sparkling Water (All Flavors)

Wegmans Brand -

Aqua Mineral Water

Italian

Lemon Flavored

Lemongrass Flavored

Lime Flavored

Frizzante European Soda

Blood Orange

Blueberry Lemon

Sicilian Lemon

Sour Cherry Lemon

Soda
- Club Soda
- Cola (Caffeine Free, Caffeine Free Diet, Diet, Regular)
- Cream Soda
- Fountain Root Beer (Regular)
- Ginger Ale (Diet, Regular)
- Grape Soda
- Green Apple Sparkling Soda (Diet, Regular)
- Tonic (Diet, Regular)
- W UP (Diet, Regular)
- Wedge Diet (Grapefruit, Peach)

Sparkling Beverage
- Black Cherry (Diet, Regular)
- Cranberry Raspberry
- Key Lime
- Kiwi Strawberry (Diet)
- Lemonade
- Mineral Water
- Mixed Berry (Diet)
- Peach (Regular)
- Tangerine Lime (Diet)
- White Grape (Diet)

Sparkling Juices
- Grape (Pink, White)

Soup

Amy's -

Black Bean Vegetable
Chunky Vegetable
Fire Roasted Southwestern Vegetable
Lentil (Light Sodium, Regular)
Lentil Vegetable (Light Sodium, Regular)

Medium Chili w/Vegetables
Split Pea (Light Sodium, Regular)
Tuscan Bean & Rice

Baxters -
Healthy Choice
Chicken & Vegetable
Puy Lentil & Tomato
Tomato & Brown Lentil
Healthy Choice Chunky
Country Vegetable

Dinty Moore - Beef Stew

Dr. McDougall's -
Black Bean & Lime
Curry Brown & Wild Rice Fruited Pilaf
Pad Thai
Tortilla

Fantastic World Foods -
Split Pea Soup
Summer Vegetable Rice

Fungus Among Us -
Organic Soup Mix
Moroccan Porcini & Green Lentil
Spicy Shiitake & Vegetable

Health Valley -
Organic
Lentil & Carrots
Split Pea & Carrots
Tomato
Organic No Salt Added
Black Bean

Lentil
Potato Leek
Split Pea
Tomato
Vegetable

Muir Glenn -
Chicken & Wild Rice
Savory Lentil
Southwest Black Bean

Pacific Natural Foods -
Curried Red Lentil

Progresso
Vegetable Classics
Garden Vegetable

Shelton's - Black Bean & Chicken, Chicken Rice

Spartan Brand - Onion Soup & Dip Mix

Thai Kitchen - Coconut Ginger (Can)

Trader Joe's -
Organic Soup
Creamy Corn & Roasted Red Pepper

Wegmans Brand -
Caribbean Black Bean
Moroccan Lentil w/Chick Pea

Spaghetti... see Pasta

Spaghetti Sauce... see Sauces

Spice... see Seasonings

Spinach... **All **Fresh** Spinach Is **Gluten/Casein/Soy-Free***

Birds Eye - All Frozen Spinach ***(Except With Sauce)***

C & W - All Plain Frozen Spinach

Cascadian Farms - Organic Frozen Cut Spinach

Del Monte - All Varieties

Freshlike - Frozen Plain Spinach ***(Except Pasta Combos and Seasoned Blends)***

Great Value Brand (Wal-Mart) -
Canned (Whole Leaf Spinach)
Frozen (Cut Leaf Spinach)

Hy-Vee - Frozen (Chopped, Leaf)

Meijer Brand -
Canned (Cut Leaf, No Salt, Regular)
Frozen Spinach (Chopped, Leaf)

Pictsweet - All Plain Spinach (Frozen)

S&W - All Varieties

Spartan Brand - Chopped, Cut, Leaf

Sunny Select - Canned, Frozen

Tasty Bite - Spinach Dal

Wegmans Brand -
Chopped Spinach (Frozen)
Cut Leaf (Frozen)
Whole Leaf

Sports Drinks

Gatorade -
Thirst Quenchers (Fruit Punch, Lemon-Lime)
Tiger Thirst Quenchers
Cool Fusion
Quiet Storm
Red Driver

Propel Fitness Water -
Berry
Black Cherry
Grape
Kiwi Strawberry
Lemon

Mandarin Orange
Peach
Wegmans Brand -
MVP Sport Drink
Blue Freeze
Fruit Punch
Grape
Green Apple
Lemon Lime
Raspberry Lemonade
Velocity Fitness Water
Berry
Black Cherry
Grape
Kiwi Strawberry
Lemon

Spread
Peloponnese -
Baba Ganoush
Dolmas
Kalamata Olive Spread
Pitted Olive & Vegetable Antipasto
Roasted Eggplant (Meze, Spread)
Sun Dried Tomato Relish
Tahini
Purity Farms - Organic Ghee (Clarified Butter)
Underwood Spreads - Deviled Ham

Sprinkles... see Baking Decorations & Frostings

Squash... **All **Fresh** Squash Is **Gluten/Casein/Soy-Free***
C & W - All Plain Frozen Vegetables
Cascadian Farms - Organic Frozen (Winter Squash)
Meijer Brand - Frozen Squash (Cooked)

S

Pictsweet - All Plain Vegetables (Frozen)

Starch

Argo - Corn
Bob's Red Mill - Arrowroot, Corn, Potato
Clabber Girl - Corn
El Peto - Arrowroot, Corn, Potato, Tapioca
Ener-G - Potato
Hy-Vee - Corn
Kingsford's - Corn
Kinnikinnick - Corn, Potato, Tapioca
Meijer Brand - Corn
Safeway Brand - Corn
Spartan Brand - Corn

Steak... **All **Fresh** Meat Is **Gluten/Casein/Soy-Free** **(Non-Marinated, Unseasoned)***

Steak Sauce

Great Value Brand (Wal-Mart)
Hy-Vee - Classic
Meijer Brand
Mr. Spice Organic - Garlic Steak
Spartan Brand - Original
Wegmans Brand

Stew

Dinty Moore - Beef

Stir Fry Sauce

Mr. Spice Organic - Ginger Stir Fry Sauce & Marinade
Wegmans Brand - Sweet & Sour

Stir Fry Vegetables

Cascadian Farm - Organic Frozen (Chinese, Thai)
Meijer Brand - Frozen Vegetable Stir Fry
Wegmans Brand - Asian, Far East, Vegetables (Hong Kong)

S

Stock

Celiac Specialties - Soup Stock (Chicken)

Kitchen Basics -

Beef

Chicken

Clam

Ham

Pork

Seafood

Turkey

Vegetable

Wegmans Brand -

All Natural Culinary Stock

Beef Flavored

Chicken

Thai

Vegetable

Strawberries... **All **Fresh** Strawberries Are**Gluten/Casein/Soy-Free***

Cascadian Farm - Organic Frozen Strawberries

Great Value Brand (Wal-Mart) - Frozen (Sliced, Whole)

Hy-Vee - Frozen (Sliced, Whole)

Meijer Brand -

Strawberries

Organic

Sliced

Whole Individually Quick Frozen

Spartan Brand - Sliced, Whole

Wegmans Brand -

Frozen (Regular, Sliced Light w/Aspartame, Sliced w/Sugar)

Woodstock Farms - Organic Frozen Whole Strawberries

Stuffing

El Peto - All Varieties

Sugar

365 Every Day Value - Brown, Raw Turbinado
365 Organic Every Day Value
Dixie Crystals - All Varieties
Domino -
Brownulated
Confectioners
Cubes
Granulated
Organic
Pure
Sugar 'N Cinnamon
Gluten Free Essentials -
Gourmet Baking Sugar
Cinnamon Vanilla
Lemon
Vanilla Bean
Great Value Brand (Wal-Mart) - Extra Fine Granulated, Light Brown, Pure Cane
Hy-Vee - Confectioners Powdered, Dark Brown, Light Brown, Pure Cane
Imperial Sugar - All Varieties
Kinnikinnick - Icing
Kroger Brand - Granulated, Light Brown
Meijer Brand -
Confectioners
Dark Brown
Granulated
Light Brown
O Organics
Publix - Dark Brown, Granulated, Light Brown, Powdered

S

Safeway Brand - Brown, Granulated, Powdered
Spartan Brand -
  Confectioners Powdered
  Granulated
  Light Brown
Trader Joe's - Brown, Organic, Turbinado
Wegmans Brand -
  Cocktail Sugar (Lemon, Mandarin)
  Dark Brown
  Granulated White
  Light Brown
Woodstock Farms -
  Organic Sugar
    Brown
    Powdered
    Pure Cane
    Turbinado

Sugar Substitute/Sweetener

Equal
Great Value Brand (Wal-Mart) - Calorie Free Sweetener
Hy-Vee - Aspartame Sweetener, Saccharin Sugar Substitute
Kroger Brand
Safeway Brand - Aspartame Sweetener
Splenda -
  Brown Sugar Blend
  Flavors For Coffee
    Caramel
    Cinnamon Spice
    French Vanilla
    Hazelnut
    Mocha

No Calorie Sweetener

Sweet and Low

Wegmans Brand -

Sugar Substitute w/Saccharin

Sweetener w/Aspartame

Sunflower Seeds... see Seeds

Sweet & Sour Sauce

LaChoy -

Lite

Regular

Mr. Spice Organic

Sweet Potatoes

Green Giant - Frozen Candied Sweet Potatoes

Meijer Brand - Cut (Light Syrup)

Swiss Chard... **All **Fresh** Swiss Chard Is **Gluten/Casein/Soy-Free***

Swordfish... **All **Fresh** Swordfish Is **Gluten/Casein/Soy-Free***

(Non-Marinated, Unseasoned)

Syrup

Dagoba - Chocolate Syrup

Hershey's - Chocolate Syrup (Lite, Original, w/Calcium)

Hy-Vee -

Butter Flavor

Chocolate

Lite

Pancake & Waffle

Strawberry

Karo - Pancake Syrup, Syrup

Kellogg's - Eggo Syrup

Log Cabin - Lite, Original

Lundberg -

Sweet Dreams Brown Rice Syrup (Eco Farmed, Organic)

Maple Grove Farms of Vermont -
Flavored Syrups
Apricot
Blueberry
Boysenberry
Raspberry
Strawberry
Pure & Organic Maple Syrup
Sugar Free Syrup
Butter Flavor
Regular
Vermont
Vermont Butter
Meijer Brand -
Butter Flavored
Chocolate
Lite Butter
Regular
O Organics - Maple Syrup
Publix - Butter Maple, Chocolate, Lite Butter Maple, Regular
Safeway Brand - Light, Original
Safeway Select - Blueberry, Pure Maple
Smucker's -
Fruit Syrup
Blackberry
Blueberry
Boysenberry
Red Raspberry
Strawberry
Trader Joe's - Maple Syrup (All)
Walden Farms -

Individual Syrup Packets (Calorie Free Sugar Free Chocolate, Sugar Free Pancake)
Syrup (Calorie Free Sugar Free Chocolate, Sugar Free Pancake)
Wegmans Brand -
Buttery Flavor (Light Reduced Calorie Pancake, Pancake)
Regular
Maple (Organic)
Maraschino Cherry Flavored
Pancake (Lite, Made w/ 2% Real Maple)
Pure Maple (Dark Amber, Regular)

T

Taco Sauce
Chi-Chi's - Taco Sauce
Hy-Vee - Medium, Mild
La Victoria - Green, Red
Ortega - Hot, Medium, Mild, Original
Taco Seasoning... see also Seasonings
Hy-Vee
Ortega -
Taco Seasoning Mix
Chipotle
Hot & Spicy
Original
Taco Shells
Meijer Brand - Taco Shells
Safeway Brand - Jumbo Taco Shells
Taco Bell - Taco Shells

T

Tahini

Peloponnese

Tamales

Amy's - Black Bean Tamale Verde

Tangerines... **All **Fresh** Tangerines Are **Gluten/Casein/Soy-Free***

Tarts

El Peto - Pecan

Glutano - Tarteletts

Tater Tots... see Potatoes

Tea

Bigelow Tea -

American Classical Tea

Darjeeling

Decaffeinated

Constant Comment

Earl Grey

English Teatime

Green Tea

English Breakfast

English Teatime

Flavored Tea

Cinnamon Stick

Constant Comment

Earl Grey

Plantation Mint

Raspberry Royale

Green Tea

Constant Comment Green

Earl Grey Green

Green Tea

Green Tea w/ (Chinese Oolong, Mango, Mint, Peach)

Herbal Tea
Berri Good
Cozy Chamomile
Mint Medley
Peppermint
Red Raspberry
Sweet Dreams
Taste of the Tropics
Tasty Tangerine
Iced Tea
Red Raspberry
Loose Tea
Constant Comment
Earl Grey
English Breakfast
Green
Celestial Seasonings -
Black Teas
Golden Honey Darjeeling
Mango Darjeeling Organic
Morning Thunder
Organic Black
Tuscany Orange Spice
Chai
Chocolate Caramel Enchantment
Decaf India Spice
Honey Vanilla White
India Spice
Cool Brew Iced Tea
Peach Ice
Green Tea

- Decaf Lemon Myrtle Organic
- Organic Green
- Tropical Acai Berry

Herbal Tea
- Acai Mango Zinger
- Bengal Spice
- Caffeine Free
- Chamomile
- Mint Magic
- Peppermint
- Red Zinger
- Sleepytime
- Sweet Clementine Chamomile Organic

Holiday Tea
- Candy Cane Lane
- Nutcracker Sweet

Rooibos Tea
- Madagascar Vanilla Red
- Moroccan Pomegranate Red
- Peach Apricot Honeybush
- Red Safari Spice

Wellness Tea
- Diet Partner
- Honey Peach Ginger
- Sleepytime Extra
- Throat Soothers
- Tummy Mint

White Tea
- Decaf China Pearl
- Vanilla Apple Organic

Great Value Brand (Wal-Mart) -
Tea 100% Natural (Decaf, Regular)
Hy-Vee -
Decaf (Green, Tea Bags)
Family Size Tea Bags
Green Tea
Green Tea Bags
Orange & Spice Specialty
Tea Bags
Thirst Splashers Raspberry Tea
Inko's White Tea -
Apricot
Blueberry
Cherry Vanilla
Energy
Honeydew
Lychee
Original
Unsweetened Hint O'Mint
Unsweetened Honeysuckle
White Peach
Lipton -
Diet Ice Tea Mix (Lemon (Decaf, Regular), Raspberry)
Regular
Green Tea Bags (Jasmine, Regular)
Instant Ice Tea (100% Instant & Decaf)
Meijer Brand -
Instant
Tea Bags (Decaf, Green, Green Decaf, Regular)
Midwest Country Fare - Tea Bags 100 Count

Newman's Own - Lemon Aided Ice Tea
O Organics - Tea`
Oregon - Match Green Tea, Original (Regular, Sugar Free)
Pacific Natural Foods -
Organic Iced Tea
Green
Lemon
Peach
Raspberry
Sweetened Black
Publix -
Tea Bags (All Varieties)
Red Rose - All Varieties
Safeway Brand - Tea Bags (Decaffeinated)
Safeway Select - Chamomile
Salada Tea - Decaffeinated & Regular (Green, White)
SoBe - Black, Green, Oolang
Spartan Brand - Green Tea
Tazo Tea - All Varieties
Trader Joe's - All Tea, Chai No Sugar Added
Twinings Tea - All Varieties
Wegmans Brand -
Black Tea
Decaf (Black Tea, Green Tea)
Earl Grey (Black, Black Decaf, Green)
English Breakfast (Black, Organic)
Green Tea
Ice Tea Mix (Decaf, Regular, w/Natural Lemon Flavor & Sugar)
Iced Tea (Lemon)
Orange Pekoe & Pekoe Cut Black Tea

T

Organic (Chai, Chamomile, Decaf Lemon Ginger Green, English Breakfast, Jasmine Green, Peppermint, Rooibos Strawberry Cream)

Teff

Bobs Red Mill - Flour, Whole Grain Teff

Tequila... **All **Distilled** Alcohol is **Gluten/Casein/Soy -Free** [2]*

Tilapia... see Fish **All **Fresh** Tilapia Is **Gluten/Casein/Soy -Free (Non-Marinated, Unseasoned)***

Tomatillos... **All **Fresh** Tomatillos Are **Gluten/Casein/Soy -Free***

Las Palmas - Crushed Tomatillos

Tomato Juice... see Drinks/Juice

Tomato Paste

Contadina - Tomato Paste

Hy-Vee - Regular Tomato

Muir Glen

Publix

S&W - Tomato

Spartan Brand - 26% Tomato

Sunny Select

Wegmans Brand - Tomato

Tomato Puree

Contadina

Dei Fratelli

Muir Glen

S&W

Wegmans Brand

Tomato Sauce... see Sauces

Tomatoes... **All **Fresh** Tomatoes Are **Gluten/Casein/Soy -Free***

C & W - All Plain Frozen Vegetables

Contadina -

Tomato

[2] www.celiac.com

Diced In Juice
Paste
Puree
Sauce
Whole peeled

Dei Fratelli -
Crushed (Regular)
Petite Diced (Regular)

Del Monte -
Diced
Basil, Garlic & Oregano
Garlic & Onion
Green Peppers & Onion
Italian Recipe
Organic
Original Recipe
Petite Cut
Regular No Salt Added
w/ Zesty Mild Green Chilies
Stewed Original Recipe

Eden -
Crushed (Regular, w/Basil, w/Onion & Garlic)
Diced (Regular, w/Basil, w/Green Chilies, w/Roasted Onion)
Whole Tomatoes (w/Basil, Regular)

Great Value Brand (Wal-Mart) -
Chili Ready Tomatoes
Concentrated Crushed Tomatoes
Diced Tomatoes in Tomato Juice
Italian Diced Tomatoes w/Basil, Garlic & Oregano
Italian Stewed Tomatoes w/Basil, Garlic & Oregano

No Salt Added Diced Tomatoes
Petite Diced Tomatoes
Whole Tomatoes In Tomato Juice

Hy-Vee -
Crushed
Diced (Chili Ready, Regular, w/Chilies)
Italian Style (Stewed)
Mild Diced & Green Chilies
Original Diced & Green Chilies
Petite Cut Diced (Regular, w/Garlic & Olive Oil, w/Sweet Onion)
Stewed
Whole Peeled

Meijer Brand -
Crushed in Puree
Diced (Chili Ready, Green Chilies, In Italian, In Juice, Organic, Regular, w/Green Chilies)
Organic (w/Basil, Whole Peeled)
Petite (Diced)
Stewed (Italian, Mexican, Regular)
Whole Peeled (No Salt, Regular)

Muir Glen -
Crushed
 Fire Roasted
 w/Basil
Diced
 Fire Roasted (Regular, w/Green Chilies)
 No Salt Added
 Regular
 Stewed
 w/Basil & Garlic

w/Garlic & Onion
w/Italian Herbs
Ground Peeled
Whole
Fire Roasted
Peeled (Plum, Regular, w/Basil)
O Organics - Canned Tomato Products
Pacific Natural Foods -
Organic
Crushed Tomatoes
Diced Tomatoes
Publix -
Crushed
Diced
Diced w/Green Chilies
Diced w/Roasted Garlic & Onion
Peeled Whole
Sauce
Stewed & Sliced
S&W - All Varieties
Safeway Brand - All Canned Tomatoes
Spartan Brand -
Diced
For Chili
Mexican
Regular
w/Green Chilies
w/Roasted Garlic & Onions)
Italian (Stewed)
Specialty Crushed
Whole

T

Sunny Select - Diced (Canned)
Trader Joe's -
Sun Dried Bruschetta
Sun Dried Tomatoes (All)
Wegmans Brand -
Crushed
Diced
Italian Style
Petite
Regular
Roasted Garlic & Onion
IC (Whole Roma)
Italian Style (Stewed, Whole w/Basil)
Kitchen Cut w/Basil
Peeled Whole
Stewed
Whole (No Salt, Regular)
Woodstock Farms -
Organic Canned Tomatoes
Crushed w/Basil
Crushed Original
Diced Basil & Garlic
Diced Italian Herbs
Diced No Salt
Diced Original
Paste
Sauce (Chunky, No Salt, Original)
Whole Peeled (Regular, w/Basil)
Tonic... see Soda Pop/Carbonated Beverages
Toppings... see Baking Decorations & Frostings
Tortilla Chips... see Chips

T

Tortilla Soup... see Soup

Tortillas

Food For Life - Brown Rice, Sprouted Organic Corn

Snyder's Of Hanover - Corn Tortillas Chips (White, Yellow)

Trader Joe's - Corn Tortillas (Original)

Trail Mix... see also Nuts

Enjoy Life - Not Nuts! (Beach Bash, Mountain Mambo)

Hy-Vee - Tropical Trail

Trader Joe's -

Almond & Cherry Mix

Antioxidant Nut & Berry Mix

Cranberry Trail Mix

Go Raw Trek Mix

Simply Spicy Almonds, Cashews & Cranberries Trek Mix

Simply The Best Trek Mix

Trek Mix... see Trail Mix

Tuna... **All **Fresh** Tuna Is **Gluten/Casein/Soy -Free (Non-Marinated, Unseasoned)***

Bumble Bee -

Prime Fillet Solid White Albacore In Water

Very Low Sodium Chunk White Albacore In Water

Crown Prince Natural -

Solid White Albacore Tuna

No Salt Added Packed In Spring Water

Packed In Spring Water

Starkist -

Gourmet Select

Solid Light Tuna Fillet In Olive Oil

Very Low Sodium

Chunk Light Tuna In Water

Chunk White Albacore Tuna In Water

Trader Joe's - Canned Tuna (All)
Tree of Life - Tongol Tuna In Spring Water (No Salt Added)
Wegmans Brand - Yellowfin Light In Water (pouch)

Turkey... see also Deli Meat ... **All **Fresh** Meat Is **Gluten/Casein/Soy-Free (Non-Marinated, Unseasoned)***

Applegate Farms -
Cold Cuts
Natural Turkey
Bologna
Herb
Honey & Maple
Roasted
Salmon
Smoked
Organic Turkey (Herb, Roasted, Smoked)

Dietz & Watson -
Turkey Breast
Black Forest Smoked
Braised Homestyle
Honey Cured
Italian Style
London Broil
Maple & Honey Cured
Mesquite Smoked
Oven Classic
Smoked Peppercorn

Hillshire Farms -
Deli Select Thin Sliced Turkey Breast
Honey Roasted
Oven Roasted
Smoked

T

Deli Select Ultra Thin Turkey Breast
Oven Roasted
Honey Roasted
Honeysuckle White -
Fresh
Breast Cutlets
Breast Roast
Breast Strips
Breast Tenderloins
Breast Thin Cut Slices
Drumsticks
Necks
Split Breast
Thighs
Wing Drumette
Wing Portions
Wings
Fresh Ground Turkey Patties
Frozen Turkey Burgers
Fully Cooked
Deep Fried Cajun Style Young Turkey
Hickory Smoked Whole (Bone In, Regular, Turkey Ham)
Oven Roasted Young Turkey
Ground Turkey
All (85/15, 97, 99% Fat Free, Burgers, Patties, Roll, Value Pack)
Marinated Turkey Selections
Chipotle Citrus Strips
Creamy Dijon Mustard Breast Tenderloins
Homestyle Breast Tenderloins
Italian Herb Rotisserie Boneless Breast Roast

Lemon Garlic Turkey Breast Tenderloins
Mild Herb Strips
Original Style Rotisserie Boneless Breast Roast
Rotisserie Turkey Breast Tenderloins
Zesty Italian Herb Breast Tenderloins
Ready To Cook
All Natural Young Whole Turkey
Fresh (Bone In Turkey Breast, Young Whole Turkey)
Frozen (Bone In Turkey Breast, Young Whole Turkey)
Spicy Cajun Style Whole Turkey
Sweet Honey Roasted Whole Turkey
Zesty Rotisserie Flavor Boneless Turkey Breast
Sausage
Bratwurst
Links (Breakfast, Hot Italian, Sweet Italian)
Patties
Roll (Breakfast, Mild Italian)
Simply Done
Bone-In Turkey Breast
Whole Young Turkey

Hormel -
Deli Sliced (Oven Roasted, Smoked)
Natural Choice Deli (Honey, Oven Roasted, Smoked)

Isaly's - Deli Meat (Oven Roasted Breast of Turkey)

Meijer Brand -
Frozen (Breast Tenders, Duckling, Split Breast, Young)
Turkey Basted w/Timer
Turkey Breast Fresh

Oscar Mayer -
Shaved Deli Meat
Oven Roasted

Smoked Turkey

Perdue -

Carving Turkey Breast

Honey Smoked

Mesquite Smoked

Deli Pick Ups Sliced Turkey (Oven Roasted, Smoked)

Deli Pick Ups Sliced Turkey Ham (Honey Smoked)

Deli Turkey

Bologna

Ham (Hickory Smoked)

Salami

Healthsense Turkey Breast Oven Roasted

Fat Free

Reduced Sodium

Rotisserie Turkey Breast

Slicing Turkey Ham

Turkey Sausage (Breakfast)

Publix -

Deli Pre Pack Lunch Meats

Extra Thin Sliced Oven

Roasted Turkey Breast

Thin Sliced Smoked Turkey Breast

Shelton's -

Free Range

Ground

Ground White

Organic (Large, Whole Small)

Whole

SPAM - Oven Roasted Turkey

Wegmans Brand - Thin Sliced Turkey Breast (Oven Roasted, Smoked)

Wellshire Farms -

All Natural Turkey Breast (Pan Roasted, Smoked)

Morning Maple Turkey Breakfast Link Sausage

Sliced (Oven Roasted Turkey Breast, Smoked Turkey Breast, Turkey Bologna, Turkey Ham)

Turkey (Andouille Sausage, Franks, Kielbasa)

Turkey Dinner Link Sausage (Jalapeno Herb, Mild Italian Style, Roasted Garlic & Parsley)

Turkey Tom Toms (Hot & Spicy, Original)

Turkey Bacon... see Bacon

Turkey Burgers... see Burgers... see Turkey

Turkey Jerky... see Jerky/Beef Sticks

Turkey Lunch Meat... see Deli Meat... see Turkey

Turnips... **All **Fresh** Turnips Are **Gluten/Casein/Soy-Free***

U

V

Vanilla Extract... see Extract

Vanilla Powder

Authentic Foods

Vegetable Juice... see Juice/Drinks

Vegetable Oil... see Oil

Vinegar

365 Every Day Value - Balsamic 5 Years Old

365 Organic Every Day Value - Balsamic

Eden -
Organic
Apple Cider
Brown Rice
Red Wine
Ume Plum
Great Value Brand (Wal-Mart) -
Balsamic
Distilled White
Premium (Garlic Flavored Red Wine, Red Wine)
Heinz -
Apple Cider ***(Except Apple Cider Flavored Vinegar)***
Distilled White
Red Wine
Hy-Vee - Apple Cider Flavored Distilled, White Distilled
Marukan - Rice Vinegar
Meijer Brand -
Balsamic Aged (4 Yr, 12 Yr)
Cider
Red Wine
White Distilled
White Wine
Nishiki - Sushi Vinegar
Publix - Red Wine Vinegar, White Distilled Vinegar
Regina -
Balsamic
Fine (Red Wine, White Wine)
Raspberry Balsamic
Safeway Select - All Varieties ***(Except Malt Vinegar)***
Spartan Brand - Cider, White

Spectrum -
Balsamic
Brown Rice (Regular, Seasoned)
Golden Balsamic
Organic (Apple Cider (Filtered, Unfiltered)
Red Wine
White Vinegar Distilled
Trader Joe's - Orange Muscat Champagne
Wegmans Brand -
Apple Cider
Balsamic (Aged Up To 3 Yrs, 8yr, 12yr)
Chianti Red Wine
Red Wine
Tuscan White
Wine
White Distilled
Vodka... **All **Distilled** Alcohol Is **Gluten/Casein/Soy-Free** 2*

W

Wafers... see Cookies
Waffles/Waffle Mix... see Pancakes/Pancake Mix
Walnuts... see Nuts
Water... **All **Pure Spring Water** Is **Gluten/Casein/Soy-Free***
Absopure
Aquafina -
Flavor Splash (Citrus Blend, Grape, Raspberry, Wild Berry)
Purified Drinking Water
Sparkling (Berry Burst, Citrus Twist)
Crystal Geyser - Alpine Spring

[2] www.celiac.com

Dasani - Regular, w/Lemon
Deja Blue - Purified Drinking Water
Evian
Fiji - Natural Artesian
Glaceau - Smartwater
Hy-Vee -
- Mother's Choice Infant Water w/Fluoride
- Natural Spring
- Premium Distilled
- Purified
- Spring

Ice Mountain
Lowes Foods Brand - Distilled, Drinking, Spring
Meijer Brand -
- Calcium
- Distilled
- Natural Calcium
- Spring

Perrier
Poland Spring - Sparkling Spring
Publix - Spring Water
San Pelligrino - Sparkling Water
Spartan Brand - Distilled, Drinking, Natural Spring, Spring
Trader Joe's - Sparkling
Wegmans Brand -
- Aqua Mineral Water Italian
  - Lemon Flavored
  - Lemongrass Flavored
  - Lime Flavored
- Nursery Water w/Fluoride
- Sparkling Water
  - Berry

Lemon
Lime
Mandarin Orange
Mineral
Mixed Berry
Spring
Regular
w/Fluoride

Whiskey... **All **Distilled** Alcohol is **Gluten/Casein/Soy -Free** [2]*

Wine... **All Wine Made **In The USA** is **Gluten/Casein/Soy -Free***

Wing Sauce

Frank's RedHot - Chile 'n Lime, Original, Xtra Hot

Worcestershire Sauce

Lea & Perrins - Original
Meijer Brand
Spartan Brand

X

Xanthan Gum

Authentic Foods
Bob's Red Mill
El Peto
Ener-G
Kinnikinnick

Y

Yams... **All **Fresh** Yams Are **Gluten/Casein/Soy -Free***

S&W - All Varieties

[2] www.celiac.com

Y Z

Yeast

Bob's Red Mill - Yeast (Active Dry, Nutritional T6635)

El Peto

Fleischmann's - Active Dry, Bread Machine

Hodgson Mills - Active Dry Yeast, Fast Rise Yeast

Red Star - Active Dry, Bread Machine

Yellow Squash... see Squash

Yogurt

Ricera - Organic Rice Yogurt (All)

Z

Zucchini... **All* ***Fresh*** *Zucchini Is* ***Gluten/Casein/Soy-Free***

Gluten/Casein/Soy-Free Over The Counter (OTC) Pharmacy Guide

Rx

Rx Allergy/Sinus/Cold/Flu Relief

Advil - Allergy Sinus, Cold & Sinus, Multi-Symptom Cold

Afrin - Nasal Spray (Original, Severe Congestion)

Airborne - Airborne Jr., Gummi Lozenges, Lemon-Lime, NightTime, On-The-Go, Original Zesty Orange, Pink Grapefruit, Power Pixies, Seasonal

Children's Motrin - Cold Suspension (Berry, Dye-Free, Grape)

Children's Tylenol -
- Cold Suspension Grape
- Plus Cold & Cough Suspension Cherry

Cold-Eeze - Cold Remedy Natural Lozenges (Cherry Flavor, Honey Lemon, Lemon Lime)

Dimetapp –
- Children's Cold & Allergy Decongestant (Yummy Grape Elixir, Yummy Grape Chewables)
- Children's Cold & Chest Congestion (Grape Syrup)
- Cold & Allergy (Elixir, Tablets)
- Cold & Chest Congestion
- Cold & Cough DM Elixir
- Long Acting Cough Plus Cold
- Non Drowsy Allergy (Tablets)
- Nighttime Flu Syrup
- Toddler's Cold & Cough Drops Decongestant Plus Cough (Great Grape)

Halls-
- Naturals (Honey Lemon Chamomile, Sunshine Citrus, Sweet Herbal Mint, Wild Cherry)
- Regular (Cherry, Ice Blue Peppermint, Mentho Lyptus, Strawberry, Tropical Fruit)

Rx

Meijer -
Apap Cough Cold (Infant Drops Cherry)
Apap PE Allergy Sinus Caplets
Apap PE Cold Flu Day Cool Caplets
Apap PE Cold Severe Congestion Caplets
Loratadine D 24hr Tablets
Nasal Spray (Liquid, Multi Symptom Liquid, No Drip Pump Liquid)
Nitetime 6 hr (Cherry Liquid, Liquid Gels, Original Liquid)
Nitetime Cough 6 hr (Cherry Liquid)
Tri-acting Nitetime Grape Liquid
Tussin (Cough Cold Softgels)
Primatene - Mist

Antacids

Lactaid - Dietary Supplement (Original Strength)
Meijer -
Antacid Calcium (XS Berry Chewables, XS Tropical Chewables, XS Wintergreen
Chewables)
Cimetidine Tablets
Effervescent Antacid Pain Tablets
Milk Of Magnesia (Mint Liquid, Original Liquid)
Pink Bismuth (Chewables, Maximum Strength Liquid, Regular Strength Liquid)
Ranitidine
Mylanta - Maximum Strength Liquid Original Flavor, Regular Strength Liquid Original Flavor, Ultra Tablets Cool Mint
Pepcid - AC 10 mg Tablets
Pepto Bismol - Caplets, Cherry Chewable Tablets, Cherry Liquid,

Rx

Max Strength Liquid, Original Liquid

Rolaids - Tablets (Cherry, Multi-Symptom Berry, Original) ***(Softchews Are NOT Gluten-Free)***

Tums -

EX 750 (Assorted Berries, Assorted Fruit, Tropical Fruit, Wintergreen)

EX Sugar Free (Orange Cream)

Regular Strength (Assorted Fruit, Peppermint) ***(Kids Cherry Blast is NOT Gluten Free)***

Smoothies (Assorted Tropical Fruit, Cocoa & Crème) ***(Assorted Fruit Smoothies, Berry Fusion Smoothies Are NOT Gluten Free)***

Ultra 1000 (Assorted (Berries, Fruit, Tropical Fruit), Peppermint)

Anti-Diarrhea

Digestive Advantage - Children's Lactose Intolerance, IBS, Lactose Intolerance Tablets

Imodium - AD Caplets, Advanced Chewable Tablets

Lactaid - Dietary Supplement (Original Strength)

Meijer -

Pink Bismuth (Chewables, Maximum Strength Liquid, Regular Strength Liquid)

Pepto Bismol - Caplets, Cherry Chewable Tablets, Cherry Liquid, Max Strength Liquid, Original Liquid

Antifungal Relief

Meijer -

Miconazole Cream (3 Day Preapp. Combo, 3 Day Disapp. Combo, 7 Day Disapp., 7 Day Reapp.)

Tioconazole 1 Day Ointment (Disapp.)

Anti-Gas

Digestive Advantage - Children's Lactose Intolerance, IBS, Lactose Intolerance Tablets
Lactaid - Dietary Supplement (Original Strength)
Mylanta - Maximum Strength Gas Mint Tablets

Cosmetics

Burt's Bees -
Healthy Treatment Parsley Blemish Stick

Cough Drops/Sore Throat Spray/Lozenges

Airborne - Gummi Lozenges
Cold-Eeze - Cold Remedy Natural Lozenges (Cherry Flavor, Honey Lemon, Lemon Lime)
Halls-
Naturals (Honey Lemon Chamomile, Sunshine Citrus, Sweet Herbal Mint, Wild Cherry)
Regular (Cherry, Ice Blue Peppermint, Mentho Lyptus, Strawberry, Tropical Fruit)
Vicks - Formula 44 Sore Throat
Lozenges (Cherry, Honey Lemon)
Spray

Hair Care

Burt's Bees -
Color Keeper Conditioner
Hair Repair Deep Conditioner
Super Shiny Grapefruit Conditioner

Rx **Dessert Essence Organics -**
Conditioner (Italian Red Grape, Red Raspberry)
Shampoo (Green Apple & Ginger, Italian Red Grape, Lemon Tea Tree, Red Raspberry)

Gluten-Free Savonnerie - All Products

Johnson's - Baby Shampoo

Meijer - Minoxidil 5% Liquid (30 Day, 90 Day)

Laxatives/Hemorrhoidal Relief

Citrucel - Fiber Therapy (Orange Regular)

FiberCon - Caplets

Meijer -
Fiber Therapy Caplets
Hemorrhoidal (Suppository)
Laxative Tablets (Natural MS, Senna)
NVP (Capsules, Original Orange Powder, Original Regular Powder, Smooth Orange Powder, Sugar Free Smooth Orange Powder)

Metamucil -
Capsules
Capsules Plus Calcium
Original Texture Fiber Powdered Drink Mix (Orange)

Lip Care

Blistex -
Lip Balm (Berry, Medicated)
Lip Infusion (Cherry, Shear, Shear Medicated)
Lip Medex
Silk & Shine

Burt's Bees -

Honey Lip Balm
Lip Balm (Tin)
Lipshimmer (All Shades)
Medicated Lip Balm

Chapstick -

100% Naturals (Botanical Medley)
Cars (Whizzin' Watermelon)
Classics (Cherry, Original, Spearmint, Strawberry)
Flava Craze
Medicated (Regular)
Moisturizer (Regular, Tube, Vanilla Mint)
Nemo (Coral Cherry, Wavy Grape)
Overnight Lip Treatment
Pirates of the Caribbean (Berry Bounty, Tropical Adventure)
Princess (Ariel Blue Coral Berry, Belle Enchanted Cherry)
Sun Care Moisturizer (Regular, Tube, Vanilla Mint)
Sun Care Ultra 30

Misc. Products

Burt's Bees -

Bug Bite Relief
Muscle Mend Rub

Cortaid - Maximum Strength Ointment

Crayola - Modeling Clay ***(Crayola Dough is NOT Gluten Free)***

Elmer's -

All Purpose Glue Stick
Glue-All Multipurpose Glue
Glue Pen
School Glue Stick

Rx **Meijer** -
Nicotine Gum (Mint, Regular)

Oral Hygiene

Anbesol - Oral Anesthetic (Baby, Canker Sore Therapy, Dentures, Junior, Maximum Strength, Regular Strength)
Aquafresh – Toothpaste (Cavity Protection)
Colgate –
Cavity Protection (Regular Flavor)
Total (Advanced Whitening, Clean Mint, Mint Stripe Gel)
Sponge Bob Squarepants (Bubble Fruit)
Crest –
Cavity Protection (Regular)
Extra Whitening
Whitening Expressions (Extreme Herbal Mint, Vanilla Mint)
Whitening Plus Scope
Glide - Floss
Listerine - Antiseptic Mouthwash (Cool Mint)
Tom's Of Maine - Natural Anticavity Fluoride Toothpaste (Spearmint, Wintermint)

Pain Relief

Advil - LiquiGels, Migraine LiquiGels, Tablets
Children's Motrin - Suspension Berry, Suspension Bubblegum, Suspension Dye Free, Suspension Grape
Children's Tylenol -
Meltaways (Bubblegum Burst, Grape Punch, Wacky Watermelon)
Suspension (Bubblegum, Cherry Blast, Grape, Strawberry)
Infant's Motrin - Drops (Dye Free, Regular)

Infant's Tylenol - Drops (Cherry, Grape)
Junior Tylenol - Meltaways (Bubblegum Burst, Grape Punch)
Meijer -
- Apap (Caplet, Cool Caplet, ER Caplet Red, ER Caplet White, ETS Tablet, Gelcap, Geltab, Tablet)
- Aspirin (Child Orange Chewables)
- Aspirin Enteric Coated (Yellow Tablet)
- Headache Tablets
- Ibuprofen (Caplets Brown, Caplets Orange, Junior Caplets, Tablets Brown, Tablets Orange)
- Migraine Caplets
- Naproxen Sodium (Caplets, Tablets)

Motrin IB - Caplets, Tablets
Tylenol -
- 8hr Caplets
- Arthritis Pain Relief Caplets
- Extra Strength Caplets
- Extra Strength Gelcaps
- Extra Strength Geltabs
- Extra Strength Tablets
- Regular Strength Tablets

Skin Care

Burt's Bees -
- Baby Bee Dusting Powder
- Bug Bite Relief
- Carrot Seed Complexion Mist
- Deep Pore Scrub
- Garden Tomato Toner
- Healthy Treatment Pore Refining Mask
- Thoroughly Therapeutic Body Butter

Rx **Coppertone** - All Varieties (Continuous Spray, Kids, Oil Free, Sport, Sunless Tanning, UltraGuard, Water Babies)
Cortaid - Maximum Strength Anti-Itch Ointment
Desitin - Original Ointment ***(Creamy Ointment Contains Gluten)***
Dessert Essence Organics -
Almond Hand & Body Lotion
Bulgarian Lavender Hand & Body Lotion
Coconut Hand & Body Lotion
Pistachio Foot Repair Cream
Pumpkin Hand Repair Cream
Spicy Citrus Hand & Body Lotion
Vanilla Chai Hand & Body Lotion
Gluten-Free Savonnerie - All Products
Lubriderm - Daily Moisture Lotion (Fragrance Free, Regular, w/ SPF 15)

Sleep Aids

Advil PM - Caplets
Simply Sleep - Caplets
Tylenol - PM Caplets

Soap

Dakota Free - Pure Prairie Soap
Gluten-Free Savonnerie - All Products
Tom's Of Maine - Body Bar (Natural Deodorant, Natural Moisturizing)

Stay Awake

Meijer - Stay Awake Tablets
Vivarin - Tablets

Supplements

Meijer -

Glucosamine & Collagen & HA
Glucosamine Chondroitin (3X, Extra Strength, Plus MSM)
Glucosamine Sulfate
Green Tea
L-Arginine
MSM 1500
Panax Ginseng
Vision Formula w/Lutein

Vitamins & Minerals

Meijer -

Calcium Coral
Ester C
Slow Release Iron
Vitamin B12

Weight Loss

Alli - Weight Loss Aid

Index

INDEX

D

E

F

Gluten/Casein/Soy-Free OTC Pharmacy

NOTES

NOTES

NOTES

NOTES

Making Gluten-Free Living Easy!

Cecelia's Marketplace

Kalamazoo, Michigan

www.ceceliasmarketplace.com

Quick Order Form

Online Orders: www.ceceliasmarketplace.com

Mail Orders: Kal-Haven Publishing
P.O. Box 20383
Kalamazoo, MI 49019
U.S.A.

Cecelia's Marketplace	Quantity	Price	Total
Gluten-Free Grocery Shopping Guide	______	(x $24.95) =	______
Gluten/Casein-Free Grocery Shopping Guide	______	(x $24.95) =	______
Gluten/Casein/Soy-Free Grocery Shopping Guide	______	(x $24.95) =	______

Sales Tax: Michigan residents please add 6% sales tax ______

Sub Total: ______

Shipping: (quantities 1-2 add $5.15)
(quantities 3-6 add $9.95) ______

Total: ______

*Please make check or money order payable to Kal-Haven Publishing

Name: ____

Address: ____

City: ____________________ State: __________ Zip: __________

Email address: ____

Making Gluten-Free Living Easy!

Cecelia's Marketplace

Kalamazoo, Michigan

www.ceceliasmarketplace.com

Quick Order Form

Online Orders: www.ceceliasmarketplace.com

Mail Orders: Kal-Haven Publishing
P.O. Box 20383
Kalamazoo, MI 49019
U.S.A.

Cecelia's Marketplace	Quantity	Price	Total
Gluten-Free Grocery Shopping Guide	______	(x $24.95) =	______
Gluten/Casein-Free Grocery Shopping Guide	______	(x $24.95) =	______
Gluten/Casein/Soy-Free Grocery Shopping Guide	______	(x $24.95) =	______

Sales Tax: Michigan residents please add 6% sales tax ______

Sub Total: ______

Shipping: (quantities 1-2 add $5.15)
(quantities 3-6 add $9.95) ______

Total: ______

*Please make check or money order payable to Kal-Haven Publishing

Name: ______________________________

Address: ______________________________

City: ____________________ State: __________ Zip: __________

Email address: ______________________________

Making Gluten-Free Living Easy!

Cecelia's Marketplace

Kalamazoo, Michigan

www.ceceliasmarketplace.com

Quick Order Form

Online Orders: www.ceceliasmarketplace.com

Mail Orders: Kal-Haven Publishing
P.O. Box 20383
Kalamazoo, MI 49019
U.S.A.

Cecelia's Marketplace	Quantity	Price	Total
Gluten-Free Grocery Shopping Guide	______	(x $24.95) =	______
Gluten/Casein-Free Grocery Shopping Guide	______	(x $24.95) =	______
Gluten/Casein/Soy-Free Grocery Shopping Guide	______	(x $24.95) =	______

Sales Tax: Michigan residents please add 6% sales tax ______

Sub Total: ______

Shipping: (quantities 1-2 add $5.15)
(quantities 3-6 add $9.95) ______

Total: ______

*Please make check or money order payable to Kal-Haven Publishing

Name: ______________________________

Address: ______________________________

City: ____________________ State: ________ Zip: __________

Email address: ______________________________